WORDS ON THE PAGE,
THE WORLD IN YOUR HANDS

BOOK TWO

Edited by

CATHERINE LIPKIN

and

VIRGINIA SOLOTAROFF

BOOK TWO

WORDS ON THE PAGE, THE WORLD IN YOUR HANDS

Prose and poetry written, selected, and adapted by contemporary writers for adults in literacy programs and others who wish to expand their reading horizons

PERENNIAL LIBRARY

HARPER & ROW, PUBLISHERS, NEW YORK
GRAND RAPIDS, PHILADELPHIA, ST. LOUIS, SAN FRANCISCO
LONDON, SINGAPORE, SYDNEY, TOKYO, TORONTO

To receive the complimentary teaching manual for *Words on the Page, The World in Your Hands,* please write to Department 361, Harper & Row, Publishers, 10 East 53rd Street, New York, NY 10022.

Grateful acknowledgment is made to Thomas M. Disch for the suggestion for the title *Words on the Page, The World in Your Hands.*

Copyright acknowledgments begin on p. 159.

WORDS ON THE PAGE, THE WORLD IN YOUR HANDS: BOOK TWO. Copyright © 1990 by Catherine Lipkin and Virginia Solotaroff. All rights reserved. Printed in the United States of America. No part of this book may be used or reproduced in any manner whatsoever without written permission except in the case of brief quotations embodied in critical articles and reviews. For information address Harper & Row, Publishers, Inc., 10 East 53rd Street, New York, NY 10022.

FIRST EDITION

Designed by Barbara DuPree Knowles

LIBRARY OF CONGRESS CATALOGING-IN-PUBLICATION DATA
Words on the page, the world in your hands/Catherine Lipkin &
Virginia Solotaroff, eds.
    p. cm.
  ISBN 0-06-055154-2 (v. 1)   ISBN 0-06-096367-0 (pbk.: v. 1)
  ISBN 0-06-055155-0 (v. 2)   ISBN 0-06-096368-9 (pbk.: v. 2)
  ISBN 0-06-055156-9 (v. 3)   ISBN 0-06-096369-7 (pbk.: v. 3)
    1. Readers for new literates. 2. American literature—20th
century. I. Lipkin, Catherine. II. Solotaroff, Virginia.
PE1126.A4W6 1990
428.6'2—dc19   88-45952

90 91 92 93 94 CC/FG 10 9 8 7 6 5 4 3 2 1
90 91 92 93 94 CC/FG 10 9 8 7 6 5 4 3 2 1 (pbk.)

CONTENTS

Contents

INTRODUCTION

José Garcia, a construction worker in his early thirties, came into a basic literacy program almost visibly trailing his shame. "I'm dumb," he said, without looking up. "I can't write." Neither could he read—in English or in Spanish, his native tongue—though he knew the alphabet, could print well, and his daughter, an alert second-grader, had started coaching him to read. He was, in fact, intelligent and ambitious, willing to come to an evening class following a workday that began at six in the morning.

At their first meeting, his tutor recorded the names of his work tools and his account of the tasks he performed with each of them. He was able to read these brief paragraphs. In meetings that followed, he spoke about his family and his school experience and was able to read an "autobiography" written in the words he had used to tell his story. His speaking vocabulary was becoming his reading vocabulary. He could soon read a simple story and, if it was in some way meaningful to him, learn its new words.

He was unable, however, to read and remember lists of unrelated vocabulary words—they meant noth-

ing to him. And he was unwilling to read primers—
"Run, Ken, run fast. You saw Igor take the money.
Now he will kill you." José was studying on tired time
and had a pressing need to learn about the real world.
He had no patience for material he felt was trivial or
meaningless.

The day he came in, tossed the "thriller" on the
library table, and said, "I'm giving this back to you," was
Martin Luther King's birthday. Copies of "I Have a
Dream" had been set out on the table. José chose King's
speech to replace the story of a boy who captured a thief
as the text for the evening's lesson.

His tutor read "I Have a Dream" aloud. She and
José discussed its themes, and together they found and
underlined its many rhythmic repetitions. As they went
through the piece again, José was responsible for reading
the refrains. They read it a third time, in unison. Then
José (with minor promptings) read the speech by himself,
although it was well above his designated "grade" level.
He was reading and understanding real writing! The
splasher was suddenly swimming, and he knew it. For
the first time he looked directly at his tutor and thanked
her for the lesson. And he took King's speech home to
read to his wife and daughter.

That experience set our minds in motion by high-
lighting a serious problem we shared with other literacy
teachers. We had very little reading material to offer our
students that in any way matched the seriousness of their
commitment to learn—not only to identify the words on

a page, that essential beginning, but to relate those words to the concerns of their lives.

Jonathan Kozel wrote *Illiterate America* in 1985. By juxtaposing the two words of his title for, perhaps, the first time, he alerted the informed public to a looming national crisis. He told us that twenty-five million American adults could not read product identification labels, menus, or street signs, and that an additional thirty-five million read "only at a level which is less than equal to the full survival needs of our society." "Together," he wrote, "these 60 million people represent more than one third of the entire adult population."

Certainly, underdeveloped reading skills are a severe vocational handicap. Just as surely, they impoverish the lives of those individuals who are thereby denied access to the information on which considered personal choices can be made. In recent years, as the social and human costs of illiteracy have come to light, government, industry, and trade unions have undertaken massive literacy programs. Their efforts have been constrained, however, by a scarcity of appropriate texts.

With few exceptions, the materials available for these programs have been written for children or have been developed by educators who, assuming that adults learn much as children do, emphasize phonics and word recognition, often at the expense of meaningful content. There is little juice or joy in a story written to incorporate a vocabulary list calibrated to early grade-level expectations. If literacy students are to experience the stimulation of thought and feeling and the strengthening of a sense of place in the human community that mature writing can engender, the texts they read must engage their adult imaginations and offer them opportunities to experience their surroundings in new ways.

How were we to provide such generative texts? We combed the literature, as others had done, and found only a handful of accessible poems and short prose passages and almost no extended work that was free of sophisticated reference, complex syntax, rare usage, or vocabulary that was well beyond the reach of inexperienced readers.

Having failed to find the texts we needed, we decided to write them ourselves. Guided by our good intentions, like others before us, we did so. We are okay writers, not good writers. We wrote okay stories, not good stories. Not good enough. Effort, pedagogical sensibility, and the best will in the world were no substitute for literary gift.

We decided to contact serious writers, several hundred of them, and ask for help. Their support for the project overwhelmed us. They responded to our suggestions, offered some of their own, and spread the word at writers' conferences. Those whose work did not lend itself to our needs suggested the names of colleagues we might contact. We are grateful to all of them. Through their generous efforts we have been able to gather the texts we wanted—good stories and poems that, in their fidelity to the ambiguity and truth of lived lives, reach out with their strange yet somehow familiar burdens. In weighted moments of recognition (for who has not lived through some version of the conflict, betrayal, innocence, joy, and despair these works contain?), they offer something we know in part, and lead us to reexamine related aspects of our own lives. Literature invites a response. In formulating that response, perceptions are sharpened, sympathies are widened, thoughts are clarified. Learning takes place.

Rather than "writing down" to their readers, the distinguished authors in the Harper & Row collections have written *to* them. Some have selected pieces from their published works, some have created original work, and others, by judicious adaptation, have made their work more widely accessible without sacrificing flavor, point, or power. One can say, then, that *Words on the Page, The World in Your Hands* represents the literary community reaching out to the literacy community by offering memorable stories, poems, and essays that challenge, enlighten, and delight.

The Editors

LIFE IS GOOD

Adapted by Garrison Keillor from his book
Leaving Home

Lightning struck the Tollerud farm Tuesday, about six o'clock in the evening. Daryl and his dad were walking the corn rows, talking, and the clouds were dark and strange but it wasn't storming yet, and Daryl said, "If I were you, I'd take Mother out to Seattle tomorrow and enjoy the trip and not worry yourself so much. I'll look after things." Right then it hit, up by the house: a burst of light and a slam and a sizzle like bacon. They ran for the house to find her in the kitchen, sitting on the floor. She was okay, but it was close. It hit a crab apple tree thirty feet from the kitchen window.

Some people in town were reminded of Benny Barnes, who was hit by lightning six times. After three, he was nervous when a storm approached, and got in his car and drove fast. But it got him the fourth time, and the fifth time it was sunny with just one little cloud in the sky and, *bam*, lightning again. He had burn scars down his legs, and his ears had been ringing for years. After the fifth, he quit running. The sixth got him sitting in the yard on an aluminum lawn chair. After that he more or less gave up. When the next thunderstorm came through, he took a long steel pipe and stood out on the hill, holding it straight up. He had lost the will to live. But just the same, it took him fifteen more years to die. It wasn't from lightning: he caught cold from the rain and died of pneumonia.

Daryl wished the bolt had come closer to his dad. His dad has something about him that drives Daryl crazy: he hates plans. The trip to Seattle was planned before Thanksgiving, letters were written to relatives, calls were made; June 30th was the date set to go. But the old man gets uneasy when plans are made and feels trapped and cornered, even if the plans are his own. So one night after chores he said, "Well, I don't know about that trip to Seattle, I might be too busy, we'll have to see about that," which made everybody else want to shoot him.

Daryl jumped up. "How can you say that? Are you crazy?" No, just nervous about plans. Always was. To agree to do something and have people expect you to do it: it bothers him. When his kids were little, he'd tell them, "Now, I'm not promising anything, but maybe next week sometime I could take you swimming, up to your uncle Carl's, but don't count on it, it all depends." As next week came around, he'd say, "I don't know about that swimming, we're going to have to see about that. Maybe Thursday." Thursday the kids would get their bathing suits out and he'd say, "We'll see how it goes this morning, if I get my work done we'll go." Right up to when they got in the car, he was saying, "I don't know. I really ought to get to work on that drain pipe," and even when he stuck the key in the ignition, he'd stop and say, "Gosh, I'm not sure, maybe it'd be better if we went tomorrow." He couldn't bring himself to say, "Thursday we swim," and stick to it. Daryl and his brothers and sisters learned not to look forward to things, because Dad might change his mind.

The old man is the same way with his grandkids. He says, "Well, we'll see. Maybe. If I can." But the Seattle trip beats all. Ruby got the train tickets and had the suitcase packed three weeks ago, then he said, "I don't know how I can leave with the corn like it is." Ruby put her head in her hands. He said, "You know, the Grand Canyon is a place I've always wanted to see, maybe we should go there." She sighed, and he said, "You know I never agreed to this Seattle trip, this was your idea from day one." Then Ruby went to Daryl's to talk to Daryl and Marilyn. They sat drinking coffee and getting madder, and Ruby said, "Oh well, you have to understand Dad." Marilyn stood up and said, "I do not have to understand him. He's crazy. He doesn't just have a screw loose, the whole top has come off."

Marilyn is reading a book, *Get Down and Garden*, about getting tough with plants. She has yanked a bunch of slow movers out of her flower garden, and it has improved her confidence. Now she often begins sentences with "Look," as in "Look, it's obvious." She used to begin with "Well," as in "Well, I don't know," but now she says, "Look. This is not that hard to understand."

She says to Ruby, "Look. It's obvious what he's doing. He wants to be the Grand Exalted Ruler and come down in the morning and hear his subjects say, 'What is your pleasure, sire?' and he'll say, 'Seattle,' so they head for the luggage and then he says, 'No, we'll stay home,' so they sit down, and then 'Grand Canyon,' and they all jump up. As long as you keep jumping, he'll keep holding the hoop up there."

Not only does Old Man Tollerud hate to commit himself to trips, he also likes to stay loose in regard to drawing up a will or some other legal paper that gives Daryl and Marilyn some right to the farm that they've worked on for fifteen years. When Daryl mentions it, his dad says, "Well, we'll have to see. We'll talk about it in a few months." Daryl is forty-two years old and he's got no more ownership of this farm than if he'd gone off and been a drunk like his brother Gunnar. Sometimes he gets so mad at the old man, he screams at him. But always when he's on the tractor in the middle of the field with the motor running. Once he left a rake in the yard with the teeth up, hoping his dad would step on it and brain himself.

Last April he saw a skunk waddling toward the barn and got a can of cat food and lured the skunk into the tractor shed, hoping his dad would start up the tractor the next morning and get a snootful. He fed the skunk day after day, waiting for it to do the job for him. Sweet justice. Blast the old bastard with skunk sauce at close range so nobody would care to see him for about

BOOK TWO   *Words on the Page,*

a year. Then the skunk started following Daryl, who fed him such rich food, so Daryl quit and the skunk disappeared.

Daryl got some satisfaction at the dinner at the Lutheran church in May, where his dad went through the buffet and loaded up and was heading for a table, when his paper plate started to collapse on him. He balanced his coffee cup on his wrist to get his other hand under the plate, and it was *hot*. The old man said, "Gosh, it's . . ." and looked for a place to dump the load; then the hot gravy burned right through the paper plate and he did a little tango and everything sloshed down the front of his pants. Daryl watched this with warm satisfaction.

But that was months ago; the satisfaction had worn off. The day after the lightning strike, Daryl drove up to the house to have it out once and for all. He practiced his speech in the pickup. "You don't treat me like I'm your son at all, you've never treated me like a son." He got to the house and found a note on the door: "Gone to Saint Cloud for windowshades. Back soon. Clean the haybarn."

Clean the haybarn! Daryl ripped the note off and wadded it up and drop-kicked it into the peonies. He marched to the end of the porch and back and stood and yelled at the door: "You don't treat me like I was your son, you bastard, you treat me like I was a —" And then the terrible truth dawned on him. His mother had said, "If anything happens to us in Seattle, I left you a letter in my dresser drawer. I've been meaning to give it to you for years." Maybe that letter said he wasn't their son. He was adopted. That's why his dad wouldn't make out the will.

Daryl had wondered about this before, if he was his father's son. He thought, "I'm forty-two, it's time to find out." He walked in and climbed the stairs, step by deep purple step, and turned and entered his parents' bedroom, the forbidden chamber, and walked to the dresser and heard something move on the bed. He turned—it was their old tabby cat, Lulu, on the bed—his hand hit a bottle and it crashed to the floor. She didn't jump at the crash; she sat up and gave him a long look that said, "You're not supposed to be in here and you know it. You ought to be ashamed of yourself. You're no good, and you know it. Shame on you." He clapped his hands— *Ha! Git!*—and she climbed down and walked away, stopped, looked over her shoulder, and said: "You'll suffer for this, you just wait."

He picked up the sharp pieces of perfume bottle and opened both windows to air out the room. Unbelievable that his mother would ever smell like this, it smelled like old fruit salads. He dug down into the dresser drawer where he'd seen her stick old pictures, under her stockings and underwear. There was a book, *Sexual Aspects of Christian Marriage: A Meditation,* by Reverend E. M. Mintner, that he'd read when he was twelve. He dug beneath it to a packet of envelopes tied with a thick rubber band, *tight.* He slipped it off: they were his dad's pay slips from the Co-op; each envelope held a year's worth; there were more than thirty envelopes.

He sat on the bed, feeling weak. Of all his parents' secrets, this was the darkest: how much money did they make? They would no more talk about that than discuss sexual aspects of marriage. One Sunday little Daryl spoke up at dinner and asked, "Dad, how much money do you make?"

His dad had several different voices—a regular one ("So how come you went down there when I told you I needed you? I don't get it") and a prayer voice ("Our Father, we do come before Thee with hearts filled with thanksgiving, remembering Thy many blessings to us, and we do ask Thee now . . ."). When he discussed money he used his prayer voice and he said, "I don't care to discuss that, and I don't want you to discuss it with anyone else. Is that clear?"

Oh, yes, we don't talk about money, that is very clear. Except to say, "I got this window fan for four dollars; it's brand-new except for this scratch, and you know those things run ten, twelve dollars." Bargains yes, but salaries no.

So here was the secret. He opened the first envelope, 1956. Forty-five dollars. That was for a whole week. Not much for a good mechanic. Forty-five dollars and five kids: it explained all that scrimping, his mother darning socks and canning tomatoes. When the old man forked over their allowance, he counted the two quarters twice to make sure he wasn't overpaying. It explained why he was such a pack rat, saving tinfoil, string, paper, rags—once Daryl looked around for string and found a box full of corks, another of bits of wire, and one box with hundreds of pieces of odd jigsaw-puzzle pieces, labeled "Puzzle: Misc."

It dawned on him that he wasn't adopted, he was their boy all right. He'd inherited their cautious natures. If his paper plate fell apart, he'd try to save it, even if his hand was burning. Same as his dad. They raised him to bear up under hardship and sadness and disappointment and disaster. But what if you're brought up to be cautious and your life turns out lucky—you're in love with your wife, you're lucky in your children, and life is lovely to you— what then? You're ready to endure trouble and pain, and instead God sends you love—what do you do? He'd been worrying about inheriting the farm; meanwhile God had given him six beautiful children. What happens if you expect the worst and get the best? *Thank you, Lord,* he thought. Thank you for sending me up here to the bedroom. It was wrong to come, but thank you for sending me.

He heard Lulu tiptoe in, and when she brushed his leg he was sorry for chasing her out. He scratched her head. It didn't feel catlike. He looked down and saw the white stripes down its back.

The skunk sniffed his hand, wondering where the cat food was. Then it raised its head and sniffed the spilled perfume. It raised its tail, as if it smelled an enemy. It walked toward the window. It seemed nervous.

"Easy, easy," Daryl said. If he opened the window wider, it might go out on the roof and find a route down the oak tree to the ground. He was opening the window wider when he heard the feet padding up the stairs. He hollered, "No, Shep, no!" and raised his leg to climb out the window as the dog burst into the room, barking. The skunk turned and attacked. Daryl went out the window, but not quite fast enough. He tore off all his clothes and threw them down to the ground, and climbed back in. The bedroom smelled so strong he couldn't bear it. The skunk was under the bed. He ran down and got the shotgun and loaded it. Daryl was almost dying of the smell, but he crept into the bedroom. He heard the skunk grunt, trying to squeeze out more juice. Daryl aimed and fired. Feathers exploded and the skunk dropped down dead.

He carried it out on a shovel and buried it, but that didn't help very much. The deceased was still very much part of the Tollerud house when his parents arrived home a little while later. Daryl sat on the porch steps, bare naked except for a newspaper. He smelled so bad, he didn't care about modesty. Ruby said, "Oh dear. Are you all right?" She stopped, twenty feet away. She thought he looked naked, but he smelled so bad she didn't care to come closer.

His dad said, "You know, Daryl, I think you were right about Seattle."

And they left. They didn't take clothes with them.

They went straight out the driveway.

That was Tuesday. Daryl has been living at his parents' house all week. But life is good. I'm sure he still believes this. Life is good, friends. It's even better if you stay away from Daryl, but basically life is good.

MOUNTAIN BLUEBERRIES

Robert Francis

These blueberries belong to birds
If they belong to anyone.
Who could have planted them but birds
Three thousand feet up toward the sun?

They live on sunshine, dust of granite,
A little rain, a little dew.
In shape a miniature moon or planet,
In color distant-mountain blue.

MOUNT KEARSARGE
❧ Donald Hall

Great blue mountain! Ghost.
I look at you
from the porch of the farmhouse
where I watched you all summer
as a boy. Steep sides, narrow flat
patch on top—
you are clear to me
like the memory of one day.
Blue! Blue!
The top of the mountain floats
above a cloud.
I will not sit on this porch
when I am old. I turn my back on you,
Kearsarge, I close
my eyes, and you rise inside me,
blue ghost.

THE LIGHT BY THE BARN

⋖§ William Stafford

The light by the barn that shines all night
pales at dawn when a little breeze comes.

A little breeze comes teasing the fields
from their sleep and waking the slow windmill.

The slow windmill sings the long day
about anguish and loss to the chickens at work.

The little breeze follows the slow windmill
and the chickens at work till the sun goes down—

Then the light by the barn again.

ROOMMATES

Adapted by Max Apple from his essay in the New York Times Magazine

Until three years ago I was a boy in relation to my grandfather. He lived to be 107 and was mentally and physically able until the end of his life. Long after the last of his friends had died, he would still go out to mow the lawn on a hot summer afternoon. His extraordinary energy never left him. I had seen it all my life: he was my roommate.

At my birth he was sixty-four, middle age to him, and he was not a gentle old soul. He argued with the men in his synagogue, screamed at his fellows in the bakery where he worked until his mid-eighties. He was a lover of strife. He enjoyed a good fight, even at a distance. When war news came on, he turned up the volume on the TV.

We never had to take care of each other, but as I learned to read, I became his teacher. When my grandfather came to the United States from Lithuania before World War I, he went to night school to learn to read and write English. Still I, the grade school scholar, considered it my duty to inform him about new things, like electricity, as he got ready for bed after a twelve-hour workday.

He was not too interested in my lectures. Within minutes he fell into a deep sleep. But even asleep there was nothing gentle about this man. He specialized in hating his enemies, even those long dead. As he talked in his sleep, he exploded in anger. From his dreams I learned the curse words of English and Yiddish. Visions of destruction crowded our room. Boils sprouted from the intestines of his enemies. Cholera depopulated their villages. The deep background of his life escaped through his lips. My young ears didn't want to listen to the uncorked anger. I didn't know what to make of feelings that could stretch back seventy years.

When I left home for college, I switched to roommates my age. Later, in graduate school, I found my own apartment, and my old roommate rejoined me. All his friends were dead. He had lived long enough to become a stranger in the community that had been his home for more than half a century. It was clear to both of us that in spite of a sixty-year age gap, I was his most congenial companion. So he joined me in the late 1960s at the University of Michigan. He made new friends, took care of himself, and did most of the housework.

Our only serious problem was what he called my laziness. I was studying for final exams. My work consisted of lying on the couch with a book in my lap. Sometimes I dozed off, now and then I highlighted a sentence with a yellow pen. He would pick up a pencil and mockingly mark his newspaper to imitate what I was doing. I could not convince him that it was work.

But I did convince others. I finished my studies, married, fathered a daughter and a son, and settled in Texas. Soon my grandfather joined us. He was exactly one hundred years older than my son.

Now that I was a man with a career, a family, and a job, I intended to help my grandfather in the last years of his life. But it turned out that I was the one who would need help. My solid life cracked in a matter of months when my wife was stricken with an incurable disease. My life became the life of the hospital. I lost touch with my friends, my work, even my children. I could not scream out my anger as my grandfather did in his sleep. Instead, I turned it against myself and it settled in my bones as depression. I went back to lying on the couch where I had studied for my exams, but I no longer saw anything glorious to underline.

So at 103 and 104 my grandfather began to take an active role in helping me care for my children. He did not understand what was happening to my wife and had no sympathy for my depression. But he saw the work of daily life in front of him and, as always, he did it. Although by then he must have been wearing the shadow of death as an undershirt, the aroma of life stayed in his nostrils. He listened to the news, he read the paper, he took out the garbage, he played with my children, he mowed the lawn. He never offered me advice or understanding; he just kept doing things.

After about two years of melancholy, I joined him. I started to see how much there was to do. Now I get up early and I stay busy. There's a lot of garbage to take out, and in Texas there's always a lawn to mow. I don't talk in my sleep yet, but even if I start nobody will hear me. Roommates like him only come along about once a century.

LOST

David Wagoner

Stand still. The trees ahead and bushes beside you
Are not lost. Wherever you are is called Here,
And you must treat it as a powerful stranger,
Must ask permission to know it and be known.
The forest breathes. Listen. It answers,
I have made this place around you.
If you leave it, you may come back again, saying
    Here.
No two trees are the same to Raven.
No two branches are the same to Wren.
If what a tree or a bush does is lost on you,
You are surely lost. Stand still. The forest knows
Where you are. You must let it find you.

NIGHT TRAIN

Robert Francis

Across the dim frozen fields of night
Where is it going, where is it going?
No throb of wheels, no rush of light.
Only a whistle blowing, blowing.
Only a whistle blowing.

Something echoing through my brain,
Something timed between sleep and waking,
Murmurs, murmurs this may be the train
I must be sometime, somewhere taking,
I must be sometime taking.

SITTING WITH MY MOTHER
AND FATHER
◂§ *Robert Bly*

My father's hard
breathing
we all three
notice.
To continue
to live
here
one must
take air.
Taking air
commits us
to sharing
air with the puma
and the eagle.

But when
breathing stops
he will escape
from that
company.
He came from
the water world

and does not
want to change
again.

My mother
is not sure
where she
wants to be,
but this
air
world
is all
she can
remember,
and neighbors
are here,
nieces
nephews,
grandchildren.

She sits
with puzzled eyes
as if to say,
where is the reckless
man who took
me from my father?
Is it this man
with gaunt cheeks
on the bed?

All those times
I drove to town
carefully
on packed snow,
is this what
it comes
to?

Yes, it is,
my dear
mother.
The tablecloths
you saved
are all gone.
The baked corn dish
you made for
your boys,
the Christmas
Eves, opening
gifts of perfume
from your husband,
they are all gone.

The nurses take
my father
for his bath.
"What sort
of flowers
are those?"

"Daisies,"
I say.
A few minutes
later you
ask again.

You and I wait
here for
Jacob
to come back
from his bath.
What can I do
but feel
time
go through me
and sit
with you?

THREE CREATION STORIES

◄§ Adapted from the Bible by Lore Segal

HEAVEN AND EARTH

In the beginning God created the heavens and the earth. The earth was without form, and empty, and the breath of God moved over the face of the waters.

God said, Let there be light, and there was light. And God saw that the light was good. And God divided the light from the darkness.

God called the light Day, and the darkness He called Night. There was evening and there was morning, the first day.

God said, Let there be a firmament between the waters, and let it divide the waters.

And God made the firmament, and divided the waters under the firmament from the waters over the firmament, and it was so.

God called the firmament Heaven. And there was evening and there was morning, the second day.

God said, Let the waters under the heavens come together in one place and let dry land appear, and it was so.

God called the dry land Earth and the coming together of the waters He called Seas, and God saw that it was good.

God said, Let the earth bear plants that have seeds, and trees that grow fruit that have seeds, each of its own kind, and it was so. The earth bore plants that had seeds, each of its own kind, and trees that grew fruit that had seeds of its own kind. And God saw that it was good.

And there was evening and there was morning, the third day.

God said, Let there be lights in the heavens to divide the day from the night, and distinguish the seasons, and mark the days and years, and let the lights shine upon the earth. And it was so.

And God made two great lights, the greater light to rule over the day, and the lesser light to rule over the night. He made the stars and set them in the heavens to shine upon the earth. And God saw that it was good.

And there was evening and there was morning, the fourth day.

God said, Let the waters swarm with living things, and let birds fly on the earth under the heavens. And God created the great monsters of the sea and every living and every creeping thing that swarms in the waters, each of its own kind, and every winged bird of its own kind. And God saw that it was good.

God blessed them and said, Be fruitful, multiply, and fill the waters of the sea, and let the birds multiply on the earth.

And there was evening and there was morning, the fifth day.

And God said, Let the earth bear living creatures. And it was so. God made wild animals of every kind, and cattle of every kind, and every kind of creeping thing, each of its own kind. And God saw that it was good.

And God said, Let Us make man in Our image, in Our own likeness, and let them rule over the fish of the sea and the birds of the heavens, and over the cattle on the earth and over the wild animals and over everything that creeps on the ground.

So God created man in His own image, in the likeness of God He created him, male and female He created them.

And God blessed them and God said, Be fruitful and multiply and fill the earth and rule over it. Rule over the fish of the sea and over the birds in the air and over every living thing that moves on the earth.

God said, Look! I give you every plant that grows on the earth, and every tree that bears fruit. They shall be your food. To every beast of the earth and every bird in the air, and to every thing that creeps on the earth and breathes with life, I have given the green plants for food. And it was so.

And God saw everything that He had made, and yes, it was very good!

And there was evening and there was morning, the sixth day.

And so the heavens were finished, and the earth,

and all the things that are on it. On the seventh day God was finished with all the work that He had done, and everything that He had made. And God blessed the seventh day and made it holy, because it was the day on which He rested from all His work and all He had created and made.

That is how the heavens and the earth were created.

ADAM AND EVE

Now on the day when the Lord God made the heavens and the earth, there was no shrub growing in the field and no plant sprouting out of the ground, because the Lord God had not yet made it rain on the earth, and there was no man to till the ground.

And a mist rose out of the ground and watered the fields, and the Lord God formed a man out of the dust of the field. Into his nostrils He blew the breath of life, and man became a living creature.

The Lord God planted a garden in Eden in the east and He took the man that He had made and put him in the garden to till it and care for it. Out of the ground the Lord God brought forth every kind of tree that was beautiful and good to eat, and into the middle of the garden He put the tree of life and the tree of the knowledge of good and evil.

And the Lord God commanded the man and said, You may eat the fruit of every tree in the garden. Eat as much as you like, except for the fruit of the tree of the knowledge of good and evil, which you may not eat, for on the day you eat it, you will have to die.

And the Lord God said, It is not good for man to be alone. I shall make him a companion, to be with him.

And the Lord God made all the beasts on the earth and all the birds in the heavens and He brought them to Adam to see what he would call them, and whatever Adam called each living creature, that was its name. But for Adam there was no companion to be with him.

And the Lord God let a deep sleep fall upon Adam. Adam slept, and God took one of his ribs and closed up the place with his flesh, and out of the rib the Lord God formed a woman, and brought her to the man.

Adam said, This is she who is bone of my bone and flesh of my flesh. She shall be called wo-man because she was taken out of man. That is why a man leaves his father and mother and becomes one flesh with his wife.

And Adam named the woman Eve, meaning Life Giver, and she became the mother of all who are alive.

And they were both naked, the man and his wife, and were not ashamed.

THE EXPULSION FROM EDEN

Now the serpent was cleverer than all the animals the Lord God had made on the earth, and he said to the woman, So you think God said you mustn't eat the fruit of all the trees in the garden?

The woman said, We may eat the fruit of all the

trees in the garden, except the tree in the middle of the garden. God said, You may not eat it, you may not touch it, or you will die.

The serpent said, You're not going to die! God only said that because He knows the day you eat that fruit, your eyes will be opened and you will be like God, and know everything, both good and evil.

The woman saw the fruit of the tree and it looked good to eat, and was beautiful, and would make her wise, and so she took the fruit and ate and gave some to her husband beside her, and he ate.

And the eyes of both were opened, and they understood that they were naked, so they braided fig leaves and covered themselves.

They heard the Lord God walking in the garden, in the cool of the day, and Adam and his wife hid from the Lord God among the trees in the garden.

And the Lord God called to Adam and said, Where are you?

Adam said, I heard You walking in the garden and was afraid, because I am naked, and so I hid myself.

The Lord said, Who told you that you were naked? Have you eaten the fruit of the tree I commanded you not to eat?

Adam said, The woman You gave me to be my companion—she gave me the fruit, and I ate.

The Lord God said to the woman, What have you done!

The woman said, The serpent tempted me, and I ate.

The Lord God said to the serpent, Because you have done this, you shall be most cursed among all the beasts upon the earth. Crawl on your stomach your life long! Eat dust! I shall make you enemies—you and the woman, and your children and her children. They will step on your head, and you will sting their heel.

To the woman He said, I shall multiply and increase the pain of your childbearing; in pain and sorrow shall you bear your children. You will yearn for your husband, and he will be your master.

To Adam He said, Because you obeyed the voice of your wife, and ate the fruit of the tree I commanded you not to eat, the earth will be cursed, because of you. In sorrow and in pain shall you get your nourishment out of the ground every day of your life. It will bear you thorns and thistles. You will eat the grain of the field; by the sweat of your brow shall you eat your bread till you return into the earth out of which you were taken, for dust is what you are and to dust you will return.

And the Lord God made tunics out of skins for Adam and his wife, and dressed them.

The Lord God said, This human has become like one of Us in the knowledge of all things, both good and evil. What if he reaches out his hand for the fruit of the tree of life as well, and becomes immortal!

And so the Lord God drove Adam out of the garden

of Eden to plow the earth out of which he was taken, and banished him from paradise. East of the garden He set angels with wheeling swords of fire to bar the way to the tree of life.

LEARNING THE WORDS

Alfred Corn

I learned the ABCs
And how to spell my name.
The letters were like trees,
No two of them the same.

I learned to spell *my life*
And lived the words I learned.
Writing the word for *knife*,
I cut myself and bled!

I spelled the word for *dove:*
One landed on the ground.
I asked the spelling of *love*,
And love is what I found.

I went where reading led;
I walked from A to Z.
I sang the words I read,
And words sang back to me.

SIX UNTITLED POEMS
From The Lark. The Thrush. The Starling.
by C. K. Williams

That the world
is going
to end someday
does not concern the wren,

it's time to
build your nest,
you build
your nest.

⋅§

This is what,
at last, it is
to be
a human being.

Leaving nothing
out, not
one star, one
wren, one tear
out.

﹏

In the middle
of a bite of
grass,
the turtle stops
to listen for,
oh, an
hour, two
hours,
three hours . . .

﹏

The fleas, too
have fled
my burned down
house. Oh,

there you are,
old friend, and
oh, you, too,
old,
old friend.

When
you were small, I
put you
in
a swing, you
held
a flower.

Next thing
I
knew . . .

You're two, that's great.
Go ahead, laugh, crawl
around.

You'll find
out,
You'll see.

ANXIETY
Linda Pastan

the grasshopper
trapped
in the wrist

is singing
its mad song
what if . . .

what if . . .
it chants
in the pause

between thunder
and flash
when you hold

your breath
to count
and knock . . . knock

goes the heart
but nobody
answers

JAPANESE INTERNMENT, 1942

Five Poems by Marnie Mueller

These poems bring to light a sad and little known period in American history. In March 1942, a few months after the Japanese bombed Pearl Harbor, 110,000 Japanese Americans—men, women, and children—were rounded up on a few weeks' notice. They had to sell their businesses, their land, and their homes—everything they owned except what they could carry in two suitcases. They were forced to gather and wait in "assembly centers." From there they were transported to "relocation camps," which were enclosed by barbed-wire fences and guarded by soldiers with machine guns.

The Tule Lake Camp I write about was built on a dried lake bed on the California-Oregon border. A wind blew almost all the time, carrying black sand. We lived there in tar-papered barracks, one family to each room, no matter how large the family. The bathrooms, outside in the center of the square, were shared by everyone. We were not allowed to eat in our own rooms, but had to go to the mess hall, where we were served food we weren't used to.

Included in this relocation center were *Issei,* Japanese immigrants who were prevented by law from becoming American citizens until 1952. There were also *Nisei,* the children of these immigrants, who had been born in the United States and so were citizens by birth. And there were *Sansei,* the third generation, who were either small children at the time or born, as I was, in the camps. My poems are written in the voices of all these people. They come from my own experience and from stories I was told as I was growing up.

SANTA ANA RACETRACK ASSEMBLY CENTER (MARCH 1942)

They put us in horse stalls.
They crowded us in,
sometimes three people
where one horse had lived.
Good enough for Japs
I guess they believed.
We found bits of manure
with straw stuck in.
Eeeouw, it was disgusting
and my mama-san cried.
She cried all day long
and couldn't be stopped
until my papa-san went out
and said he wouldn't come back.
After that she banged her head

against the side of our stall,
like a horse that's gone mad
I heard some people say.
Like a horse gone mad
mama-san banged her head
in front of the strangers
we were penned in with.

TRAIN RIDE TO TULE LAKE INTERNMENT CAMP (MAY 1942)

We were riding all night on the train,
all night on the train,
all night, with the shades pulled down,
and the lights turned out.

I lean against mommy,
I lean my head in her lap,
I lean against mommy all through the night.
The only lights are two little red ones
in the front and the back of the car.

When I open my eyes in the middle of the night
I can see heads shaking,
bobbing, swaying,
I can see heads
of our neighbors in the dim red light.
I have my coat on, it's cold in the train,
my blue Easter coat, my new-bought one.

They called us dirty Japs
and mommy didn't dare
let us go to church
on White River Street.

So my coat is brand-new on the train,
on the train to I don't know where.

FIRST WEEK AT TULE LAKE

Papa won't talk
not one single word
no matter what mama says.
"Papa-san, you stop that,"
she says. "You be a man.
Your children cry.
Your children ashamed."
But papa only sits by the window
and stares out.
He doesn't move the whole day.

We bring him food
from the mess hall—
American food
like in my school back home,
not so bad, I think.

He turns and looks
when I give it to him.
For a minute it seems like
he's going to smile—
his mouth goes up that way.
Instead he spits
fat and disgusting
right in the middle of the tin plate.

TEENAGE BOY AT TULE LAKE

Mama measured me
today, I grew one more inch.
Papa grew smaller.

ISSEI BACHELOR AT TULE LAKE

It good to be bachelor here,
no children
to see your shame.

SURVIVOR

Sally Ann Drucker

A Polish Jew
during World War Two
I moved as fast
as borders changed.
I changed disguise
as borders moved.

I moved so fast
barefoot on ice
I never felt the cold
until the Russian army
came to set me free;
I had no time to feel
I never felt the cold.

ALL DAY
✍ *Dennis Brutus*

All day I wear an opaque mask,
but at dawn I wake
my eyelids wet
with tears shed in dreams

SIGN LANGUAGE

An old tale retold by Blanche L. Serwer-Bernstein

In the land where I was born, our rulers were so cruel even the stories we told revealed that we did not feel safe among them. We liked to tell our children the many ways we found to outwit their wicked plots against us, so that our community could live in peace. This is one of our stories.

One day, not so very long ago, our honored leader, whose name was Solomon, was summoned by the ruler of the land to come at once to the palace. When Solomon was standing before him, the ruler glared down at him with terrible eyes and began to speak:

"I challenge you to a contest in sign language," he said in a loud, commanding voice. "Let one of your people come forward, and I will speak to him with gestures and signs. You must find someone among you who can understand what I mean and can answer correctly in my sign language. If he fails, he loses the contest and also his life."

Our leader's heart pounded. His face turned pale.

Who could meet such a challenge? What man could understand the ruler's secret language?

"I give you thirty days to choose someone and prepare him for this test," continued the ruler. "If nobody comes forward to accept my challenge, all of you will die." Then the ruler drew his head back and smiled a terrible smile.

Solomon, our brave leader, trembled with fear and anger, and went home deeply troubled. He sent word to all the people in the village to gather in the house of prayer, and there he told them of the ruler's wicked scheme. He explained that one of them must accept the challenge to understand and to answer in a sign language only the ruler knew.

"One of you must risk your life," he told them, "otherwise all of us will perish."

Not a man among them thought he was wise enough to accept the ruler's challenge. One week passed, then two. Three weeks went by, but no one came forward. Meanwhile the devout prayed night and day, asking for a miracle so that their people would not be destroyed.

When the thirty days were almost up, Joseph the poultry dealer returned to the village from a long trip, bringing with him a great many chickens he had bought from the farms nearby. He went directly to the market to sell his fine birds but was surprised to find that every shop was closed. Then he heard the murmur of many voices praying.

"Oh," he blushed, "have I forgotten? Is this a holy day?"

He hurried to the prayer house, where he found his wife, Sarah, praying with all the others.

"What on earth is the matter?" asked Joseph.

Sarah turned her frightened eyes toward him. "The cruel ruler has demanded that one of us must come to speak with him in a sign language only he knows. If the man we send fails to understand and to answer correctly, he will die. Worse still, if no one of our people meets the challenge, all of us will die."

"Is that what all the wailing and praying is about?" asked her husband in amazement. "Well, I'm ready to take up the challenge. Go to our leader and say that I, Joseph the poultry dealer, will compete with the mighty ruler in his cunning sign language."

"And what do you know about sign language, my husband? How will you understand him?" asked the good Sarah.

"What are you worried about? If no one volunteers, we all will die. What do I lose by taking up the challenge? Perhaps this way I shall be able to save my people, my children, and you, my dear wife. For me, it is worth a try."

Sarah trembled. Surely Joseph must fail in his brave attempt to save his people from the wicked ruler who wished them all dead. Even so, Sarah loved her husband for his courage, and she trusted his good sense.

At last she agreed that Joseph should take the risk. Together they went to find Solomon.

"O wise leader," said the poultry dealer, "let me be the one to answer the cruel ruler in his cunning sign language."

Solomon looked at him for a long time. At last he spoke. "Bless you, my son. May God be with you both, Joseph and Sarah."

Finally, the day of the contest arrived. Everyone gathered in the village square. A man in a red cloak blew on a golden trumpet as the mighty ruler entered the square and climbed up to his high throne.

The ruler looked down on all his people. He roared with laughter when he saw that it was the lowly poultry dealer who had taken up his challenge. "Does such an ignorant fellow really think he can answer my clever sign language?" he said, wiping tears from his eyes.

"Joseph, do you understand what you must do?" he asked.

"I guess so," said Joseph, in a voice so low that the people had to press forward to hear him.

"Remember, O master of chickens"—the ruler laughed—"you must watch the signs I make and you must understand exactly what they mean. Then you must answer me in the same way, so clearly that I understand your message."

"I know what I must do," replied Joseph.

Everybody waited, hardly breathing; the competition was about to begin.

The ruler stood up and raised one finger. He held it high above his head and turned all around so that everyone could see it.

Without hesitation, Joseph raised *two* fingers, and showed them to all the people.

The ruler's face turned white. How had this ignorant fellow been able to answer him? The contest was not going as he had expected it to. He tossed his head and tried to smile, as if to say, "That first test was much too easy."

Then the ruler took a slab of yellow cheese from his pocket. He held it up, smelled it, and let a look of pleasure come over his face, so that the people would know that it was sweet and delicious.

Joseph the poultry dealer answered him at once by taking an egg from his own pocket and holding it up for all to see.

Although the ruler was amazed at Joseph's response, he had no choice. He had to go on with the contest. He took a handful of grain from his pocket and scattered it on the floor.

At that, Joseph smiled, opened his poultry coop, and set a hen free. The hen wandered all about and gobbled up every single seed.

The ruler was by this time astonished. He called out in a loud voice to all the people:

"This man has matched my every sign!
He won the match. Now let us dine
on bread and cake and fish and wine
and dates and figs. This treat is mine!"

Everyone rejoiced to see the challenge end so happily. But no one understood the ruler's signs or Joseph's responses.

The people crowded around Joseph. They all tried to speak at once. "How did you know what to do?" they said, their eyes wide with wonder.

"It was simple," Joseph explained. "You saw the ruler point at me with one finger, meaning to take out my eye? Well, I pointed to him with two fingers, showing that 'If you do, I will take out both your eyes.'

"Next he held up a piece of cheese. He meant to show that I was hungry and he was not. So I took out an egg to let him know that I did not need his charity.

"Then he scattered some grains of wheat on the floor. I decided to feed my hen. She was hungry, and I thought it would be a pity to waste the grain."

At the very same time, the ruler's friends gathered around him. "What did your signs mean?" they asked him in puzzled voices.

The ruler told them his side of the story.

"First I pointed one finger, meaning that there is only one king. But the poultry dealer pointed two fingers, meaning that there are two kings, one in heaven and one on earth.

"Next I took out a piece of cheese, meaning to ask, 'Is this cheese from a white goat or a black?' Now, that was a very hard question, which I did not expect him to answer. But he took an egg from his pocket to answer me with *his* question: 'Is this egg from a white hen or a brown?'

"Finally, I scattered some grains of wheat on the floor, meaning to show him that his people are spread all over the world. Then the poultry dealer answered me by freeing his hen, who ate up all the grain to let me know that the Messiah will come to gather God's faithful children from wherever they are scattered on the face of the earth.

"Did you ever think a poultry dealer would be so clever?"

THE GOOD SAMARITAN

A parable told by Jesus
(from the Book of Luke, Chapter 10),
translated from the Greek by Morton Smith

Once, when Jesus said, "You are to love your neighbor as yourself," a man asked, "Who is my neighbor?"

Jesus, in reply, said:

"A man went down from Jerusalem to Jericho and fell in with thieves, who, when they had stripped and beaten him, went off, leaving him half dead.

"It happened that a priest was going down that road and saw him and went past on the other side.

"Similarly a Levite, coming to the place and seeing him, went past on the other side.

"But a Samaritan going along came upon him and pitied him and, going to him, bandaged his wounds, pouring on oil and wine, and put him on his own donkey and brought him to an inn and took care of him.

"And the next day he took out two silver coins, gave them to the innkeeper, and said:

" 'Take care of him, and whatever you spend beyond this I shall give you when I come back.'

"Which of these three seems to you to have been the neighbor of the man who fell in with the thieves?"

He said, "The one who showed him mercy."

Jesus said to him, "You go and do likewise."

GETTING INVOLVED

❧ Adapted from his story "I Love New York" by Madison Smartt Bell

All over the pages of the New York *Post* there are pictures and stories of people starting to get involved. I'm always seeing headlines like

SUBWAY RIDERS CAPTURE BANDIT
HOLD TILL COPS ARRIVE
or
WOMAN K.O.'S CON MAN WITH BRICK
or
CITIZEN NABS TIMES SQUARE MUGGER

Things are looking up in New York City. The *Post* just reported the passage of a tough new gun law. Death by violence will now decline. In the opinion of this newspaper, everything is going to get real nice real soon. I hope they're right.

The other day I went out to see a double feature. When the movies were over I was hungry and stopped at Ray's on Prince Street for an Italian sausage with green peppers and grease baked in pizza dough. They call this a SoHo Roll, for some reason I don't know, and it costs $1.65. Anyway, I didn't feel hungry anymore after I had eaten it all.

Across the street beggars were sleeping sweetly in the mouth of a burned-out building. It was late and everything was quiet. Everything was as it should be, or at least as it usually is. I walked through garbage and broken glass over to the Bowery and stopped for a traffic light.

Across the Bowery two bums were fighting in a doorway. Two bums are always fighting in doorways on the Bowery at half-past midnight, and no one ever takes any interest. But as I watched from my corner I thought I detected signs of malicious intent, and I decided to cross over and poke my nose in.

This I began to do. But the light was still red, and when I got to the middle of the street, cars were streaming uptown and I had to wait for the line to go by. Meanwhile the action in the doorway seemed to be taking on the shape of a mugging.

A big man and a little man were wrestling. The little man was wearing a tan suit coat. While I stood there looking over the stream of cars, the big man forced this coat down over the little man's elbows and finally took it away from him altogether. Then he began to walk up the street, holding the coat by the collar, shaking it, dipping his hands into the pockets.

Meanwhile the last car in the line stopped at my feet. I looked and saw that it was a police car. There was a pair of cute young cops inside, just like the ones on TV. "Hey," I said, pointing, "there's a mugging taking place right across the street!" The light changed, and the police car went in gear and shot off uptown at sixty miles an hour. This was disheartening.

I could now get across the street, but that magic moment when I might have prevented a crime had passed while I was stuck behind the traffic.

The mugger and his victim were now walking up the street, with a little distance between them. It offended me to see the mugger strolling along. If you are going to rob someone, you might have the decency to run away afterward. I followed behind, keeping my eyes on the two of them. They were about to pass a parking lot enclosed in a chain-link fence. Guard dogs run behind the fence at night. They maul you first and ask questions later. By the time the mugger got to the parking lot he had finished with the coat. He threw it over the fence and kept on walking, whistling now and swinging his arms. The little man stopped by the parking lot and stood watching the dogs eat his coat. He looked very unhappy. I passed him without saying hello.

I kept following the mugger, who I had decided was someone to dislike. He turned into a bar near the corner. I have been in the bar many times. There is a small pool table, and sometimes I go and play for dollar bills with the bums and small-time criminals who hang out there. It is a good place to hustle dollar bets but probably not a good place to make a citizen's arrest. As I walked past, I took a good look at the mugger through the grimy plate glass and saw him settle in at the bar. I walked on to the phone booth on the corner and punched the police emergency number, 911.

A woman's voice answered. "Hello," I said. "I just saw a mugging on the Bowery, and the guy who did it went into a bar here and I think he might be there for a while."

"Can you describe the perpetrator?" she said.

"No," I said. "I'll describe me. I'm a white male with short brown hair and a black jacket with a hole in the back and a brown shoulder bag. I'll be waiting for the car on the corner of Bowery and Houston." I hung up.

During the two and a half minutes I was on the phone, a fight had broken out in the bar, and when I came back it was all over the street. It was a bums' fight, a lot of shouting and not much real contact. I didn't see the perpetrator, and I wasn't sure if he was still inside or not. I stood on the corner for seven minutes. Then the car with the same two cute cops in it pulled up. "Fella, we didn't see any mugging," they said. "All we saw was two guys walking down the street."

"Why didn't you talk to me?" I said.

"So," the cops said, by way of an answer, "can you describe the guy you say did something?"

"Sure," I said, and I did. Then I said, "I think he's in the bar across the street."

The cops looked across at the bar with less interest than I had expected. The fight was over, and everybody was going back inside. "Yeah. Well, what about the other guy?

"Him?" I said. "He's older, a little guy, middle-aged. Has on dark pants and a white shirt, straight hair with a bald spot in the back. He must have gone the other way or I would have seen him pass."

"Hey, I think we know that guy," said one of the cops. "We better drive around and see if we can spot him."

"You want me to wait for you to come back?"

"I wouldn't do that if I were you," they said. "It isn't altogether safe around here." The squad car pulled out and headed off downtown.

The next day I was still worked up. I told my girlfriend what had happened on the Bowery. "So?" she said. "This is the city. Things happen. Your problem is you don't *do* anything. You should get to work and stop sitting around being depressed." She's usually right.

I decided to get to work on my depressing apartment. For one thing, I had cockroaches in my telephone. Whenever I made a call, some roaches would roll out from under the dial, like tiny paratroopers bailing out. I had mice too, in the kitchen. One day I saw a mouse that was so big it was almost a rat. When I shooed at it, it just sat there giving me this "what are *you* doing here" look. Then it slouched off under the sink. I set out for Canal Street to get some poison.

I checked the subway trash bin and found a New

York *Post* to read. When the train came, I got on the first car and stood at the door so I could look down the tunnel. It gives me a kind of high and makes me forget things. After a few minutes I walked back and took a seat and opened my *Post*. There was a large picture of a teenager being arrested on suspicion of robbing subway passengers. SUSPECT MUGS FOR CAMERA, the paper said. The suspect, in a model's pose with one hand on her hip and the other handcuffed to a transit officer, was giving us a big smile. She had on short shorts and a T-shirt that said I LOVE NEW YORK. A notice on the same page informed riders that subway tokens were going to cost more on the first of July.

By the time I came out of the subway it was pouring rain. I had on cloth shoes, so my feet got wet and I was probably going to catch cold. I thought I would just buy the other papers there at the corner, go home, get in bed, and read them.

There were a lot of people crowded under the awning of the newsstand to get out of the rain, and all of them were pushing me. There was a cop leaning over the counter asking for a copy of *Consumer Reports*. A Latin woman was trying to get his attention.

"Someone is just now taking my purse," she was saying, "with my cards and my money." She was about four feet tall and wore a damp cotton sack dress.

The cop dodged away from her and went to the other end of the counter. The woman followed him. "My cards and all my money," she said. "Also my umbrella, which I am buying only today."

"Go to the precinct and report it," the cop said. He turned to the newsboy. "Gimme a copy of *Consumer Reports,* the one with the '88 cars in it."

The woman went out and stood on the corner. Raindrops gathered in her hair. I went up to her. "Do you still see him?" I said.

"Yes, yes," she said, and pointed. "He is there with my cards, my money, and my umbrella, which is new. I do not know where is the precinct."

On the other side of Canal Street there was a young Latin guy in a hurry. "You're sure about this?" I said.

"It is my new umbrella he is holding now in his hand. My purse he has thrown already away. But my cards and my money, those he still must have."

The light changed, and I trotted across the street. I caught up with the guy by the vacant lot on the next corner. He had a short Afro and a dirty blue windbreaker. In his right hand he was holding a folding umbrella of the kind you buy for two dollars on any street corner ten minutes before it rains. The umbrella was shut.

I once studied karate for several years, though I have never done any street fighting. I took no time to consider. If I considered, I knew I would do nothing. As it was, I hit the guy on the left shoulder with the heel of my hand, hard enough to spin him. He came around very quickly, swiping with the umbrella. I stepped outside and hit his wrist with a single-arm block, and the umbrella flew away somewhere. Now his left hand was coming toward my face, but slowly enough that I could catch it. I held his hand, turned it up and inward in a loop that puts pressure on the wrist, the elbow, and the shoulder. A guy I met in the park once showed me this particular trick, which is supposed to be unbearably painful.

The alleged purse snatcher went to his knees on the wet sidewalk. "Aaah," he said. "You must be crazy, bro."

I didn't stop. I had forgotten why I was doing this, but I didn't seem to be able to stop. Rainwater was running out of my hair into my eyes and mouth. I remembered about the umbrella and turned my head to look for it. The Latin woman was stumping along toward us on her swollen wet feet. I watched her pick up the umbrella.

"Is not my umbrella," she said. "My umbrella was with flowers." She came closer, bent over, and peered at the stranger I was torturing on the sidewalk. "Is not the same one," she said, "is not the same."

I didn't feel up to apologizing. I let go the guy's hand and stepped back out of range. He stood up, thought it over, and split. I pulled my hair as hard as I could and started back to Canal Street. The woman was waddling behind me. She was talking, but to herself, I think, and not to me.

"Is not the same one," she said regretfully, "not the same. They are all looking the same now, the young people." I heard the umbrella pop open. "Is not so bad this umbrella," she said, "though it is not so beautiful as the other. But it is keeping off the rain. I go now to the precinct to tell of my cards and my money."

I decided to walk home across the Brooklyn Bridge to take my mind off what had happened. I climbed the stairs to the walkway. When I came to the first tower, the rain had stopped and the sky began to clear. I looked down at the street below the bridge. All the people were coming out onto the street now that the rain was over. The people were no bigger than cockroaches, and it was true that they did all look the same. Also when I put my hand out over the railing, my hand covered all the people up and I couldn't see any of them anymore.

BUMS AT BREAKFAST
David Wagoner

Daily, the bums sat down to eat in our kitchen.
They seemed to be whatever the day was like:
If it was hot or cold, they were hot or cold;
If it was wet, they came in dripping wet.
One left his snowy shoes on the back porch
But his socks stuck to the clean linoleum,
And one, when my mother led him to the sink,
Wrung out his hat instead of washing his hands.

My father said they'd made a mark on the house,
A hobo's sign on the sidewalk, pointing the way.
I hunted everywhere, but never found it.
It must have said, "It's only good in the morning—
When the husband's out." My father knew by heart
Lectures on Thrift and Doggedness,
But he was always either working or sleeping.
My mother didn't know any advice.

They ate their food politely, with old hands,
Not looking around, and spoke in short plain an-
      swers.
Sometimes they said what they'd been doing lately

Or told us what was wrong; but listening hard,
I broke their language into secret codes:
Their *east* meant *west,* their *job* meant *walking and
walking,*
Their *money* meant *danger, home* meant *running
and hiding,*
Their *father* and *mother* were different kinds of
weather.

Dumbly, I watched them leave by the back door,
Their pockets empty as a ten-year-old's;
Yet they looked twice as rich, being full of break-
fast.
I carried mine like a lump all the way to school.
When I was growing hungry, where would they be?
None ever came twice. Never to lunch or dinner.
They were always starting fresh in the fresh morn-
ing.
I dreamed of days that stopped at the beginning.

WHERE HE WAS:
MEMORIES OF MY FATHER

Adapted by Raymond Carver from his essay "My Father's Life"

My dad's name was Clevie Raymond Carver. His family called him Raymond, and his friends called him C. R. I was named Raymond Clevie Carver, Jr. I hated the "Junior" part. When I was little my dad called me Frog, which was okay. But later, like everybody else in the family, he began calling me Junior. He went on calling me Junior until I was thirteen or fourteen. Then I told them all that I wouldn't answer to that name any longer. So he began calling me Doc, or else Son.

The day he died I was away from home. My mother telephoned my wife with the news. When my wife answered the phone, my mother cried out, "Raymond is dead." For a moment my wife thought that *I* was dead. Then my mother made it clear which Raymond she was talking about, and my wife said, "Thank God. I thought you meant *my* Raymond."

My dad walked, hitched rides, and rode boxcars when he went west across the country from Arkansas to Washington State in 1934, looking for steady work at decent pay. Out in Washington, he picked apples for a time, and then he landed a construction worker's job on the Grand Coulee Dam. After he had put aside a little money, he went back to Arkansas to help his folks, my grandparents, pack up for the move west. He said later that in Arkansas they were about to starve. It was during that short time, while he was back in Arkansas, that my mother met my dad on the sidewalk as he came out of a tavern.

"He was drunk," she said. "I don't know why I let him talk to me. His eyes were glittery. I wish I'd had a crystal ball." He had had girlfriends before her, my mother told me. "Your dad always had a girlfriend, even after we were married. I never had another man. He was my first and last. But I didn't miss anything."

My parents, this big, tall country girl and a farm-hand turned construction worker, were married by a justice of the peace on the day they left for Washington. My mother spent her wedding night with my dad and his folks, all of them camped by the side of the road in Arkansas.

Out in Omak, Washington, my dad and mother lived in a little place not much bigger than a cabin. My grandparents lived next door. My dad went on working on the dam. It was dangerous work, and some of his friends had died there. Later, when the dam was finished, my father stood in a crowd and heard President Franklin D. Roosevelt speak right there at the construction site. "He never mentioned those guys who died building that dam," my dad said.

Then he took a job in a sawmill in a little town in

Oregon. I was born there in Clatskanie, and my mother has a picture of my dad standing in front of the sawmill, proudly holding me up to face the camera. My bonnet is on crooked and about to come untied. His hat is pushed back on his forehead, and he is wearing a big grin. These were his salad days.

In 1941 we moved to Yakima, Washington, where my dad went to work as a saw filer, a skilled trade. When the war broke out, he wasn't called up to the army because his work was considered necessary for the war effort. Lumber was in demand by the armed services, and my father kept his saws so sharp they could shave the hair off your arm.

At that time, my dad moved his folks into the same neighborhood, and by the mid-1940s the rest of his family—his brother, his sister and her husband, as well as uncles, cousins, nephews, and most of their families and friends—had come out from Arkansas. All because my dad came out first. The men went to work at Boise Cascade, where my dad worked, and the women found jobs packing apples. In just a little while, it seemed, everyone was better off than my dad. "Your dad couldn't keep money," my mother said. "Money burned a hole in his pocket. He was always doing for others."

The first house I can clearly remember living in, at 1515 South Fifteenth Street in Yakima, had an outdoor toilet. On Halloween night, or just any night, for the hell of it, neighbor kids, kids in their early teens, would carry our toilet away and leave it next to the road. My dad would have to get someone to help him bring it home. After a while, though, everyone went to indoor plumbing until, suddenly, our toilet was the last outdoor one in the neighborhood. I remember the shame I felt when my third-grade teacher, Mr. Wise, drove me home from school one day. I asked him to stop at the house just before ours. I told him I lived there.

I can recall what happened one night when my dad came home late, to find that my mother had locked all the doors on him from the inside. He was drunk, and we could feel the house shudder as he rattled the door. When he managed to force open a window, she hit him between the eyes with a heavy metal strainer and knocked him out. It was as heavy as a rolling pin, and I used to pick it up and imagine what it would feel like to be hit in the head with something like that.

I remember my mother pouring his whiskey down the sink. Sometimes she'd pour it all out and sometimes, if she was afraid of getting caught, she'd only pour half of it out and then add water to the rest. I tasted some of his whiskey once myself. It was terrible stuff, and I didn't see how anybody could drink it.

We finally got a car in 1950, a 1938 Ford. But it threw a rod the first week we had it, and my dad had to have the motor rebuilt.

"We drove the oldest car in town," my mother said. "We could have had a Cadillac for all he spent on repairs." One time she found a tube of lipstick on the floorboard, along with a lacy handkerchief. "See this?" she said to me. "Some floozy left this in the car."

Once I saw her take a pan of warm water into the bedroom where my dad was sleeping. She took his hand from under the covers and held it in the water. I stood in the doorway and watched. I wanted to know what was going on. This would make him talk in his sleep, she told me. There were things she needed to know, things she was sure he was keeping from her.

In 1956, the year I was about to graduate from high school, my dad quit his job and took a job in Chester, a little sawmill town in northern California. The reasons he gave at the time for taking the job had to do with a higher hourly wage and some talk that he might, in a few years time, be given the job of head filer. But I think, in the main, that my dad had grown restless and simply wanted to try his luck in a new place. Also, the year before, within six months of each other, his parents had died.

After graduation, when my mother and I were packing to join him in Chester, my dad penciled a letter to say he'd been sick for a while. He didn't want us to worry, he said, but he'd cut himself on a saw. In the same mail we got an unsigned postcard from somebody down there telling my mother that my dad was about to die and that he was drinking "raw whiskey."

When we got down to Chester, my dad was living in a trailer that belonged to the company. I didn't recognize him immediately. He was skinny and pale and looked bewildered. His pants wouldn't stay up. He didn't look like my dad. My mother started to cry. My dad put his arm around her and patted her shoulder, like he didn't know what this was all about, either. The three of us took up life together in the trailer, and we looked after him as best we could. But my dad was sick, and he couldn't get any better.

I worked with him in the mill that summer and fall. We'd get up in the mornings and eat eggs and toast while we listened to the radio, and then go out the door with our lunch pails. We'd pass through the mill gate together at eight in the morning, and I wouldn't see him again until quitting time. In November I went back up to Washington to be with the girl I'd made up my mind I was going to marry.

The following February, my dad collapsed on the job and was taken to the hospital in Chester. Now, in addition to being physically sick, he was in the midst of a nervous breakdown, though none of us knew to call it that at the time. I went down and drove him and my mother back up to Washington. During the entire trip he didn't speak, not even when we asked him a direct question. He'd communicate, if he communicated at all, by turning his head or by turning his palms up as if to say he didn't know or care. The only time he said anything on the trip, and for nearly a month afterward, was when I was speeding down a gravel road and the car muffler came loose. "You were going too fast," he said.

Back in Yakima, a doctor saw to it that my dad went to a psychiatrist. My mother and dad had to go on relief, as it was called, and the county paid for the psychiatrist, who put him on the fifth floor of the Valley Memorial Hospital and began giving him electroshock treatments.

I was married by then and about to start my own family. My dad was still locked up when my wife went into the same hospital, just one floor down, to have our first baby. After she had delivered, I went upstairs to give my dad the news. They let me in through a steel door and showed me where I could find him. He was sitting on a couch with a blanket over his lap. *Hey,* I thought. *What in the hell is happening to my dad?* I sat down next to him and told him he was a grandfather. He waited a minute and then said, "I feel like a grandfather." That's all he said. He didn't smile or move. He was in a big room with lots of people. Then I hugged him, and he began to cry.

Somehow he got out of there. But now came the years when he couldn't work and just sat around the house trying to figure out what next and what he'd done wrong in his life that he'd wound up like this. My mother went from job to crummy job. Much later, she spoke of that time he was in the hospital, and the years just afterward, as "when Raymond was sick." The word *sick* was never the same for me again.

He'd been off from work for six years and had lost everything in that time—home, car, furniture, and appliances, including the big freezer that was my mother's pride and joy. He'd lost his good name too—Raymond Carver was someone who couldn't pay his bills. His self-respect was gone.

In 1964, through the help of a friend, he was lucky enough to be hired on at a sawmill in Klamath, California. He moved down there by himself to see if he could hack it. He lived there in a one-room cabin, not much different from the place he and my mother had started out living in when they went west.

During those years I was trying to raise my own family and earn a living. But, one thing and another, we found ourselves having to move a lot. I couldn't keep track of what was going on in my dad's life. But I did have a chance one Christmas to tell him I wanted to be a writer. I might as well have told him I wanted to become a plastic surgeon. "What are you going to write about?" he wanted to know. Then, as if to help me out, he said, "Write about stuff you know about. Write about some of those fishing trips we took."

Then he died. I was a long way off, in Iowa City, with things still to say to him. I didn't have a chance to tell him goodbye, or that I thought he was doing great at his new job; that I was proud of him for making a comeback.

My mother had a photograph of my dad during those early days in Washington. He is standing in front of a car, holding a beer and a stringer of fish.

In the photograph he is wearing his hat back on his forehead and has this awkward grin on his face. I asked her for it and she gave it to me. I put it up on my wall, and each time we moved, I took the picture along and put it up on another wall. I looked at it carefully from time to time, trying to figure out some things about my dad, and maybe about myself in the process. Finally, in the course of another move, I lost the photograph. It was then that I tried to recall it, and at the same time try to say something about my dad, and how I thought that in some important ways we might be alike. For one thing, I found myself, like him, having trouble with alcohol. My writing was a way of trying to connect up with him.

The night my father died my mother said he came in from work and ate a big supper. Then he sat at the table by himself and finished what was left of a bottle of whiskey, a bottle she found hidden in the bottom of the garbage under some coffee grounds a day or so later. Then he got up and went to bed, where my mother joined him a little later. But in the night she had to get up and make a bed for herself on the couch. "He was snoring so loud I couldn't sleep," she said. The next morning when she looked in on him, he was on his back with his mouth open, his cheeks caved in. *Gray-looking*, she said. She knew he was dead—she didn't need a doctor to tell her that. But she called one anyway, and then she called my wife.

After the service at the funeral home, after we had moved outside, a woman I didn't know came over to me and said, "He's happier where he is now." I stared at this woman until she moved away. I still remember the little knob of a hat she was wearing. Then one of my dad's cousins—I didn't know the man's name—reached out and took my hand. "We all miss him," he said, and I knew he wasn't saying it just to be polite.

I began to weep for the first time since receiving the news. I hadn't been able to before. I hadn't had the time, for one thing. Now, suddenly, I couldn't stop. I held my wife and wept while she said and did what she could to comfort me there in the middle of that summer afternoon.

I listened to people say consoling things to my mother, and I was glad my dad's family had turned up, had come all that way to where he was. I heard our name used a lot that afternoon, my dad's name and mine. *Raymond*, these people kept saying in their beautiful voices out of my childhood. *Raymond.*

ABANDONED FARMHOUSE
Ted Kooser

He was a big man, says the size of his shoes
on a pile of broken dishes by the house;
a tall man too, says the length of the bed
in an upstairs room; and a good, God-fearing man,
says the Bible with a broken back
on the floor below the window, dusty with sun;
but not a man for farming, say the fields
cluttered with boulders and the leaky barn.

A woman lived with him, says the bedroom wall
papered with lilacs and the kitchen shelves
covered with oilcloth, and they had a child,
says the sandbox made from a tractor tire.
Money was scarce, say the jars of plum preserves
and canned tomatoes sealed in the cellar hole.
And the winters cold, say the rags in the window
    frames.
It was lonely here, says the narrow country road.

Something went wrong, says the empty house
in the weed-choked yard. Stones in the fields
say he was not a farmer; the still-sealed jars

in the cellar say she left in a nervous haste.
And the child? Its toys are strewn in the yard
like branches after a storm—a rubber cow,
a rusty tractor with a broken plow,
a doll in overalls. Something went wrong, they say.

THE RETARDED ANGEL

◄§ Stephen Dunn

Wordless with a message,
you sit on our shoulders
off-balance, one wing

apparently useless,
haunting us
like a father

who won't judge
his son's sullen
deliberate wish

to be judged.
Other angels have urged us
to change our lives,

but you seem to know
we drift, stumbling
toward even the smallest

improvement. To see you
is to imagine how long
and with what difficulty

it took you to reach us,
years perhaps
of landing elsewhere.

Whoever sent you
must have been desperate
and accidentally brilliant, you

with whom we'd never argue,
the damaged, unnerving,
barely hopeful last resort.

(After George Dennison)

THE PRODIGAL SON

A parable told by Jesus
(from the Book of Luke, Chapter 15),
translated from the Greek by Morton Smith

A man had two sons, and the younger of them said to his father, "Father, give me my share of the property."

So he divided his estate between them. And not long after, the younger son, collecting everything he had, went away to a distant country and there wasted his property, living wastefully.

When he had spent everything, a severe famine occurred in that country, and he began to be in want.

So he went and attached himself to one of the citizens of that land, who sent him into his fields to feed pigs, and he wished he could make a meal of the husks the pigs were eating, and nobody gave him anything.

So, coming to himself, he said:

"How many of my father's servants have more food than they need, and here am I, dying of hunger! I shall get up and go to my father and say to him:

" 'Father, I have sinned against heaven and against you; take me as one of your servants.' "

So he got up and went to his father. While he was still far off, his father saw him and pitied him and, running, fell on his neck and kissed him.

The son then said to him:

"Father, I have sinned against heaven and against you; I am no longer worthy to be called your son."

But his father said to his slaves, "Quick. Bring out the best clothes and clothe him, and put a ring on his hand and shoes on his feet. Bring the fatted calf, sacrifice it, and we shall eat and rejoice, because this my son was dead and has come back to life, he was lost and has been found!"

So they began to have a party. His elder son, however, was in the fields.

When, coming home, he got near the house, he heard singing and dancing. He called one of the boys and asked what was this.

The servant said to him, "Because your brother has come, and your father has killed the fatted calf to celebrate because he got him back safe."

Then he was angry and did not want to go in. But his father, coming out, begged him to. So he answered and said to his father:

"Look how many years I have been serving you, and I never broke one of your rules, and you never gave me a little goat so that I could have a party with my friends.

"But when this son of yours, who ate up your property with whores, came back, you killed the fatted calf for him."

But his father said to him:

"My child, you are always with me, and all that I have is yours. But we ought to be glad and rejoice, because this your brother was dead and has come back to life—was lost and has been found."

TALE

❦ Rosellen Brown

Joe and Maddy Jones were home when the bad
news came: Uncle Tucker had gone and done it—
checked out, passed over, crossed the line, kicked the
bucket, sailed on home. They never really knew him; he
was on the fancy side of the family (the one that had a
funeral home, and then ten funeral homes, with big ads
in the paper that said: LET TUCKER TUCK AWAY YOUR LOVED
ONE!). So they weren't too sad.

But Maddy called out "Joe!" when she read the
letter about Tucker's own funeral and how the mayor
came, and the best and richest folks. "He's gone and left
us a gift!" And so he had, and a big one—$1,500—just
for being in the family.

They called everyone to tell them. "Poor dear
Uncle Tucker, he was always such a kind man, taking
care of his own!" Now they were sad *and* glad.

You'd think the check was made of glass, the way
they held it when they went to cash it. Then, first thing,
they started to argue about what to spend it on.

Maddy wanted a sofa that didn't sag and a new rug,
a washer that worked and some warm clothes for win-

ter—the kids were too big for everything in the closet. Joe had other ideas that mostly had to do with a car, or else a stereo, a pair of slick boots for himself, and for his Maddy, a dress he saw in a store window that would hug her hips and make her look like a queen. They lay in bed and dreamed and argued and dreamed and argued. Maddy said, "I wish we could send Uncle Tucker a thank-you note in heaven."

"Wait a long time, you can deliver it by hand," Joe said, and Maddy kicked him hard.

But when they woke, this is what happened:

They got a call from Maddy's sister in Alabama— "Oh, come on home, darlin', your old grandma is dying!" And Maddy had to go. She took the train and stayed awhile to help and sing and pray, and came on home when Grandma was better. But as soon as she got home old Grandma gave in and died after all, and this time Maddy took a plane to get there fast to say goodbye and took the children with her.

Then Joe's brother had a hospital bill and Joe had to pay it,
and while he was in the hospital, someone stole everything in his house that had an electric plug, and they had to buy him a few things so he wouldn't be so upset that he'd have to go back to the hospital,
and then the baby set fire to his mattress and Maddy thanked the Lord he only burned his blanket and got him a new bed, super deluxe, flameproof,

and then the Welfare said, "No checks from us—
you have all this *money!*"

and then Maddy broke her glasses falling (but
saved her nose) and needed new ones,

and her sister Cat needed the rent because her
man was gone and needed some milk for the twins who
were always hungry and had a lot of teeth at three
months,

and then Joe's friend Rex got in a little mess with
the law and needed bail (until he could pay him back.
"Don't hold your breath," Maddy told him, "or you'll
die blue in the face!"),

and then her sister Rose Bell's children had no
coats and boots to go to school in the snow and they *had*
to go to school, so she got them coats and boots and
mufflers too, all the same flame red so they could mix
and match if someone lost something,

and then Erroll, their oldest boy, was going to graduate and he had to rent a cap and gown (but he did look
fine),

and then the lady next door (who lost her leg a long
time ago when she met a train on a dark dark night)
needed a new leg to keep up with the times and the
insurance gave her about enough to buy the foot,

and the shelf that held the dishes fell down and
they had to get a new set, plastic this time so they'd
never break,

and then Joe got sick and missed a lot of work and
the bills piled up,

and soon they were going to have to borrow money from someone, if anyone had any.

Maddy lay down next to Joe. She no longer dreamed about how to spend Uncle Tucker's gift; they no longer argued. All she could do was smile a little in the dark because they were all alive.

"Joe," she said, and reached over and took her husband's nice warm hand. "I'd still like to send Uncle Tucker a thank-you note. But what in the world do you think I could tell him?"

MEDICINE

◄§ Carolyn Kizer

The practice of medicine
Is not what it was
In my grandfather's time.

I remember him telling me
Of weeks that went by
When he would be paid
Only in chickens
Or only potatoes;

Of treating the families
Of striking miners
In Montrose or Telluride
Who could not pay at all;
Of delivering babies
(A total of twenty)
For a tribe of dirt farmers
Who paid one new-laid egg
Or a cup of spring water:

After sweating a breach birth,
And twins at that,

At five in the morning
It was mighty good water.

When, fifty years later
He came back to the mountains
Middle-aged babies
Ran up in the street
Crying, Doc! Doc! eyes streaming,
Tried to kiss his old hands.

No, the practice of medicine
Is not what it was,
But it has its moments:

That morning in surgery
I regained consciousness
A little too early
And found the doctor
Kissing my hand,
Whispering, whispering,
It's all right, darling,
You're going to live.

for W. S., MD

THE MECHANIC

*Adapted by Pam Conrad
from her story "The Mechanic"*

I was so light then that when I jumped on the heavy rubber cord that ran from the gas pumps, I couldn't make the raspy *ding* sound in the office. And I was still so young that when I walked across the station and into the garage, the other mechanics didn't gawk at me. I must have been ten or eleven.

It was winter, and the two huge doors to the garage were rolled up. The wind whipped in but could not disturb the heaviness inside: stacked batteries, shelved tires, and fan belts and steering wheels racked against the walls, all covered with a greasy black dust that smelled of gasoline.

My eyes searched the tar-like darkness inside, and the wind pushed me through the door. Scotty, the owner, nodded as he walked past me in his green work suit, just like my father's, but clean. Walking deeper into the garage, I stepped over lifts that jutted out of the floor on huge steel cylinders, slippery shafts that I had seen rise powerfully out of the ground. I liked them. I would have touched one, pressed my cheek against the cold steel, except that my mother had warned, "Watch out, they might sink." "Watch out, they might spring up." But I knew they moved slowly, lifting heavy cars effortlessly into the air.

I stepped around machines with gauges and clamps and dials worn with abuse. I ducked under hanging belts and saw my father's hips and legs over a fender, the rest of him deep under the hood of a shiny gray car. His feet jerked in response to some straining and pulling that he was doing inside.

A girl at school told me about a mechanic who had been fixing his car when the hood fell down on him and crushed him dead. She knew my father was a mechanic. Now I touched my father, his leg, and looked at the heavy, yawning hood balanced open at an angle I couldn't trust. "Hi, Daddy."

Twisting, he looked back at me. "Be with you in a minute, sweetie. Almost done." He chose some pliers from a pile of tools laid out on a rag draped across the fender. "Why don't you wait in the office? There's a heater in there."

"Nah. That's okay."

"Suit yourself." Banging, twisting, clanging. He slid off the fender and came round to the front of the car, tugging things. "How was your ballet class?"

"Good."

"Practice hard?"

"Un-huh."

I sat down on a wooden crate and pulled my bag up on my lap—my ballet slippers, my leotard.

"What do you mean, 'un-huh'? If you want to be like Maria Tallchief, you've got to practice hard, every day, and with enthusiasm."

"I'll never be like her, Daddy. I'm not an Indian."

"Oh? You're not an Indian?" He smiled and flicked a dirty rag at my head. It didn't touch me, but it shot a fine burst of soot over my face.

"Daddy!" When I said *Daddy* in that tone—with a slight whine—it would mean, Oh, you're so dumb, you don't understand a thing, you're hopeless. I wiped my sleeve over my face and rubbed my fist into my eyes.

He stood looking at me, wiping his dirty hands on a black rag. He was still smiling. It embarrassed me, the way he thought I was so special. I knew I wasn't; I'd been in school and around other kids long enough to know that. But the way he looked at me, I knew he was loving the sight of me in my winter coat, with my ballet gear, sitting there on a wooden crate in his garage. "You look nice."

"Oh, Daddy." Now I laughed.

He turned back to his work. "Okay. Let's see if we can get home." He faced the car, released the hood, and slammed it down. Spreading his feet and throwing back his head, he pressed his powerful arms and hands down onto the hood, and bellowed, "Thy sins are forgiven thee. Rise up and walk, you bomb."

There was laughter from the guys up front as he turned and climbed into the car. It started right up, filling the air around me with a roar and thick fumes. He winked at me through the windshield, turned the motor off, and got out.

"Boy, am I good!" He kissed the top of my head as he walked by. "Follow me."

At the sink in a back corner, he sprinkled green powder on his hands and scrubbed them with a brush as he talked.

"There's something you should always remember, Elizabeth." He called me that when he was angry or very serious. Green-black bubbles dropped from his hands, and I stood closer to him, leaned on him.

"Yeah?"

"It's important you remember this in all you do— ballet dancing or whatever."

"What's that?"

The skin on his hands was beginning to show through the grease. He added more soap. "It's this: attention to detail separates the amateur from the professional, and the professional from the artist."

I looked up at his face, his smart, thoughtful face. "What does that mean?"

"Well, it means when you're an amateur at something—a beginner—you just worry about the main thing, the large parts of what you're doing. But as you get more experienced, you start to pay attention to the smaller parts, the details. Then you're a professional. But if you take it one step further, go beyond what's necessary, care about the smallest details . . . ah, then!"

He looked at me meaningfully, drying his hands. *"Then you are an artist!"*

I loved him like that, talking ideas to me like I was a grownup. I loved the fan belts hanging there in front of him, the edges of his heavy undershirt around his wrists, the grime on his hands that wouldn't come off, stains that said he was a car healer.

We held hands and left together. He called out goodbye to the men standing around by the Coke machine, and they yelled back, "So long, Professor," and laughed. They didn't understand my father; they just didn't understand about being an artist.

FOLDING A SHIRT

Denise Levertov

Folding a shirt, a woman stands
still for a moment, to recall
warmth of flesh; her careful hands

heavy on a sleeve, recall
a gesture, or the touch of love;
she leans against the kitchen wall,

listening for a word of love,
but only finds a sound like fear
running though the rooms above.

With folded clothes she folds her fear,
but cannot put desire away,
and cannot make the silence hear.

Unwillingly she puts away
the bread, the wine, the knife,
smooths the bed where lovers lay,

while time's unhesitating knife
cuts away the living hours,
the common rituals of life.

CHICKEN NOTES

Adapted by Roy Blount, Jr., from his book
One Fell Soup

I think there is more to the chicken than it gets credit for. The chicken is as close to man and as savory as the apple, as full of itself as the lion or the rose. A hen's feathers feel downy but organized when you lift her up. She has a peck like a catcher's snap throw to first. A chicken never makes eye contact with a person. Who is to say why it crosses the road?

It is hard, however, to discuss the chicken seriously. It is possible to talk about even the sheep seriously, or the badger; but most people cannot consider "the chicken" for sixty seconds without something in the back of their minds going *"Booo*-uk buk buk," dipping its head suddenly and pecking a bug. So I will not try here to get to the bottom of the chicken. I will just set down one person's Chicken Notes.

WHICH FIRST, CHICKEN OR EGG?

This is one of those questions like:

Do the same tastes really taste the same to different people?

or

If you could get inside another person's head, would you know it, or would you think you were the other person?

One of those questions, I mean, that people have been wanting the answer to since early childhood.

Okay. No one will ever track down an eyewitness account of that exact moment when one or the other, the chicken or the egg, came first. It is up to each of us to decide. I say the chicken. If an egg were first, the chances are that Adam, Eve, one of the beasts of the field, even one of the beasts of the air, would have eaten it. Or at least stepped on it. But a chicken can run. The chicken was first, I believe, and it stayed alive long enough to lay several dozen eggs. Also, if the egg came first, what fertilized it? In point of fact, the egg must have come third.

At any rate, talking about chickens gets us back to basics.

ON FRIED CHICKEN
Goodness; Eating

My mother's (rolled in flour and dropped in *hot* shortening in a *hot, heavy* iron skillet, at *just* the right time, for just the right *length* of time) is not only the best fried chicken but also the highest form of eating. It is crisp, not crusty. In the best fried chicken, you can't tell where the crust leaves off and the chicken begins. Sure,

I have read about caviar and pheasant under glass and would not deny them a place at my table. But in my thoughts they do not crunch, give, tear, or ooze the way well-fried chicken does.

By the way, when chicken is fried right, the tastiest meat of all is between the small bones of the breast: chicken rib meat. I have never heard anyone mention this meat. I have never spoken of it myself, even privately, until now. Fried chicken is a personal experience, like the woods out beside your house, so another thing I recommend is to go off alone with a small roasted chicken to explore all its crisp and juicy parts. You get to know a chicken that way. But look for the rib meat. It's worth the trouble.

I also like chicken meat that offers some resistance. Meat should be earned, at both ends. Chickens themselves are resourceful eaters. Remember in the comic strip *Smilin' Jack* the fat sidekick who was followed around by a chicken that ate his shirt buttons as they popped off?

KEEPING CHICKENS
A Personal Account

One Easter, when I was about thirteen, I got a baby chick that had been dyed pink. Now, I believe that dying chicks and ducklings is wrong. But this chick thrived and made a good pet. Some people don't believe this, but before all the pink had grown out of it, this chicken was already running around the yard after me like a puppy.

I used to carry it around in my shirt or in my bicycle basket. (I am not going to say what its name was. You can't win, telling what you named a chicken. The reaction will be either "That's not a funny name for a chicken" or "He had a chicken with a funny name. Big deal.") I didn't love it the way you love a dog or a cat, but I really liked it, and it liked me. We were talking about that chicken the other day. "I would think that would be embarrassing, being followed by a chicken," said my brother-in-law Gerald.

"No," said my sister Susan, "that chicken liked him."

But the chick grew into a pullet. We had no place to keep a grown chicken. At our previous house we had kept six chickens in and around a chicken house, and my father was softhearted about wringing their necks—that is, he would try to wring their necks in a softhearted way. As I recall. When I asked my mother for details, she wrote:

> *The chicken house was there complete with rather sad-looking and unproductive chickens when we bought the house. There was a rooster and five hens.*
>
> *The people we bought the house from had them because of the war and food shortage. I was sorry they were there. Daddy was glad. You were delighted with them. The chicken house smelled so*

*bad nobody wanted to clean it. We finally decided
two eggs a week were not worth it. The chickens
didn't look any too healthy; then, too, they had
names. After one try we decided we couldn't eat
them, and gave them to the coal man.*

*The one try was by Daddy. He assured me he
could kill a chicken. His mother had always wrung
their necks, and he had watched. He violently
wrung this chicken's neck real hard and threw it on
the ground. It lay stunned and then wobbled drunk-
enly off to the chicken house. We spent the rest of
the week nursing it back to health.*

When the chickens were gone, the chicken house
remained. It was made of scrap lumber and tar paper. I
used it as a fort and a clubhouse until I was eleven or
twelve and started playing ball.

My mother hated the chicken house. She said it
ruined our backyard. She burned it down by accident,
she said. One afternoon she was raking leaves and burning them, and the fire spread to the chicken house. Mrs.
Hamright, across the street, was out watering her
bushes. She smelled smoke and heard the sirens coming.
Her reflex was to yell "Oh dear Lord" and squirt the
hose through the window of her house onto her husband,
Gordy, who was reading the paper. We had to give him
our copy of the evening paper. Even though *we* were the
ones who'd had the fire.

Mr. Lovejohn, the old man who lived next door to the Hamrights, came over in his dark-brown suit about the same time the firemen started thrashing around with their hoses. He said he wanted to "counsel" with us. He said the fire was the wages of smoking in bed.

"Now, Mr. Lovejohn," my mother said. "No one in our family smokes, anywhere. And there aren't any beds in the chicken house."

"That don't excuse it," he said.

By the time the firemen got there, the chicken house was about gone, but they stretched the hoses all over the yard, trampled a dogwood tree, and eyed our house as if they would love a chance to break some windows. We didn't have many fires in our area at that time of year. The guys in the fire department liked to set fire to unwanted buildings on purpose and put them out for practice, playing the fire along for hours at a time, if they could.

My parents didn't want to go through all that again, so we gave my pet chicken to Louisiana, who came every Wednesday to iron and clean and yell, "You better not *bleev* that man, child," at the female characters in the soap operas. She received a lot of things we didn't know what to do with. My chicken was getting too big; I could see that. Having a grown chicken for a pet would have been a strange thing.

"How's the chicken?" Susan and I would ask Louisiana every Wednesday.

"He wa— He's *fine,* " Louisana would say. Finally, when we said we wanted to visit it, she said she had let it go to see her granddaughter who lived eighty miles away.

"Does she play with it lots?" we asked.

Louisana said she did.

HOW TO HAVE FOURTH OF JULY
Jonathan Holden

Use a sledge to smash each burlapped
bale of ice into wet jewels. With
whiskey-soaked mint leaves picked
that morning, pack this ice
into tall glasses until
you can scrape the frost off
with your nail. Pour on
the bourbon, drink
till your ears ring, your teeth
ache. Drink till your lips
are numb and you smell
the summer rain in a field filled
with fresh, wild mint.
      Never dunk cherry-bombs.
Under water they'll only go
boink! Light them on land,
where their flash breaks the air
in half, bursts it like
a big bag, leaving scorched edges
torn and smoking.
      When you slaughter the watermelons,
break off such hunks that when

you bite in you get water
all up your nose.
    And when it gets dark, don't go
to the fireworks. Go out into
sweet, cool thickets of
darkness, chase
the fireflies.
Clap them in jars until each jar
is inlaid with sleepy stars.

WATERMELONS
◦§ Charles Simic

Green Buddhas
On the fruit stand.
We eat the smile
And spit out the teeth.

CAR WASH

*◆§ Adapted by Sylvia Tennenbaum
from her story "Car Wash"*

When Esther Hepplewhite's husband died, suddenly and unexpectedly, on a Tuesday morning in the dentist's chair, people in town wondered how it would affect the dentist's business. They knew that Esther didn't have to worry; she was well fixed. But that nice young man might have a rough time. "Not that we blame *him,*" they all said, knowing full well that they would never set foot in his office again.

Esther had good teeth, but she had other problems. Melvin had left her with two cars. The 1986 silver-gray Chevy had been hers—it even said HERS on the license plates—and the 1989 Chrysler LeBaron had been HIS. She sold the Chevy and kept the Chrysler. It had whitewall tires, electric windows, air-conditioning, a radio, and a tape deck on which she played her favorite tunes. It was too bad about the HIS on the license plates.

Widowhood was not easy for Esther Hepplewhite. She was fifty-seven and no longer a spring chicken, even if she had kept her shape by watching her diet, getting enough sleep, and bearing no children. Men used to joke with her and flirt a little when Melvin was alive. Now that she needed them, they looked the other way. Her dresses got shorter, along with those of other women, and she had her hair done every week. But she found it hard to talk to strangers, and her friends never seemed to have much time for her when she called them on the telephone.

She kept up by reading book reviews and going to movies. She played gin rummy and canasta, and took good care of her house. She decorated the bedroom to suit herself (Melvin had not allowed lacy frills or feminine colors) and gave all the HIS towels to the Goodwill. She volunteered to drive old people to their doctors, but that got her down, so she collected money for the Red Cross instead.

Still, something was missing in her life. It was Melvin, of course, even though she found it hard to recall his face. To keep his memory alive, she set out a photograph of him in each room of her house. Her friends thought it was weird, but she was comforted by the pictures. It was as if he guarded her, and they reminded her that she had been a faithful wife.

Now that she was without a husband, Esther was no longer invited to parties. Her friends treated her like a time bomb that might go off at any moment and take one of their husbands with her.

"You should go to Atlantic City," they said to her, "or maybe on a nice cruise?"

So she went to a hotel in the Catskills, but all she got for her money was a bad cold from the steam bath. Her nose and eyes dripped, and she looked a mess. The

only men who showed an interest in her were twin brothers. One of them repeated, like an echo, what the other
said, and they both believed that the Russians were
messing with the weather.

Then she discovered the car wash.

The boy who used to do the car for her had gone
off to college, so that she had to take the LeBaron to the
car wash on Route 25. The first time she went, on a lazy
spring morning, there wasn't even a line. When she
drove up, she noticed half a dozen young men hanging
about, not paying much attention to her as she sat there.
She beeped her horn lightly—what she thought was a
friendly sound—and one of the men strolled over. He
was skinny, with a little beard showing on the bottom of
his chin.

"Shut your windows, lady," he said, "and drive on
nice and slow, until I tell you to stop."

Esther smelled whiskey on the man's breath, but
she smiled sweetly and pressed the buttons to shut all the
windows real tight. He turned the water on and sprayed
her car from top to bottom and from side to side. It was
like being in a cloudburst, and when it stopped she saw
that two more men had come over and were getting ready
to wash her car all over. One of the men had a black rag
on his head, and the other wore a sweatshirt that said
PEACE NOW.

All together now, the men started to slap soapy
cloths and sponges and frothing mops against the car's

body. Esther felt a thrill up and down her spine with every thump and splash. She saw the men's faces dimly through the soapy windshield. They were without expression. Only their jaws moved on some chewing gum, and their hands were busy rubbing the white walls, sponging the windshield, and soaping down the hood in long, easy strokes. They worked quickly, gracefully, swishing the rags gently around the headlights.

All she could hear was the sound of the sponges, like steps on a soft carpet. It was warm inside her car. It felt just lovely to be getting washed. Better than anything had felt in a long time.

They washed the rear end and gave the HIS license plate a dab or two and gently swabbed the antenna with a sponge. They took a long soapy rag between them and ran it over the roof. Her scalp tingled a little. One of the men bent down and slowly rubbed the front bumper, back and forth, back and forth, and he made a little circle around the front license plate. He stroked the hood, easy now, and leaned across her fender and wiped down her window once again.

My, thought Esther, what a careful, gentle young man.

Then all at once the men stood back up against the wall. The one with the black rag around his head turned a switch, and while the white lather slowly sank down the windshield and left little snowy pathways and popping bubbles, Esther was once more swept up in a storm. Water crashed against the sides and top of the car. It was thrilling, like being in a waterfall, but still snug and safe in her car. A lovely sensation came over her.

Then it was all over, and she saw that the men had walked away, all but the one with the scraggly beard, and he was motioning her to drive out, back into the sunshine. She sighed contentedly and gave him a little wave with her hand. It wasn't until he opened the car door and a cool breeze wafted across her knees that she noticed how hot it was inside the car.

"Do the seats and the floor?" he asked, his eyes never leaving her face. Esther moved back. Yes, there was whiskey on that man's breath—or maybe just beer.

"No, thank you just the same, not today," she said in her old-lady voice.

The three others returned to dry the car, but the drying wasn't up to the washing, just a few pats with big damp towels that weren't very clean. The proprietor, chewing on the stump of a cigar, came over to collect the money. "Three dollars," he said.

"Your sign outside says two-fifty," Esther told him.

"That's without tax," he answered. "Read the fine print."

Esther saw it was useless to argue. The man handed her a pink card with one hole punched in it. "Each time you come here," he said, keeping the cigar in his teeth, "ask us to punch it, and you'll get a free wash when the card is full."

Esther gave him a big smile, even though she felt cheated. She slipped the card in her purse. She just wanted to get home now and take a nice nap. Too late, she noticed the white plastic bleach bottle that had *Tips for the Boys* written on it. "Next time," she thought, "next time I'll give *them* a dollar."

That night the LeBaron gleamed in the light of the full moon. It was still clean the next day, but the day after, she thought she found some dust on the hood and a few mud splashes on the fenders, so she drove to the car wash and had them do another great job. It was Friday and they were charging four dollars, but that didn't matter to a widow left well fixed by her husband. May his soul rest in peace.

Every few days, when the sun shines, Esther Hepplewhite drives out to Route 25 to the car wash, to let the men rub her car down again. They must know it's not dirty—the white-wall tires shine and it always comes in spotless—but they look coolly through the suds swirling on the windshield and the rivers of clean water pouring down the glass, which make Esther's face appear lined and wobbly. They look and rub and chew calmly on their toothpicks. Their dark eyes don't let on a thing.

HIGH FUNGOES

I am hitting fungoes to my sons,
lazy loops into September's afternoon.

Hit me a popper, dad.

I am hitting high fungoes to my ranging sons,
who catch them.

They are catching the ball:

One-handed, shoestring,
over the shoulder, driving in,
my babies are catching high fungoes
in September's afternoon.

They peg the ball across the field,
a bullet at my heart,
throwing straight and hard.
The ball bursts like cannonade.
I sting my hands.

Hit me a popper, dad. Hit one to me.

And I swing in a low, aching arc like a club
against the blue marine doom
of high September, hitting out and out
in the afternoon
as my sons leap up like airy nets
snagging every desperate drive,
circling easy under the ball
surprised by gravity.
I swing again and again
until there is nothing I can knock over or beyond
    them.

CLOTHESPINS
ᴥᏕ Stuart Dybek

I once hit clothespins
for the Chicago Cubs.

I'd go out after supper
when the wash was in
and collect clothespins
from under four stories
of clothesline.
A swing-and-a-miss
was a strikeout;
the garage roof, Willie Mays,
pounding his mitt
under a pop fly.
Bushes, a double;
off the fence, a triple;
and over, a home run.
The bleachers roared.
I was all they ever needed
for the pennant.
New records every game—
once, ten homers in a row!
But sometimes I'd hit

the clothespins
so hard they'd explode,
legs flying apart in midair,
pieces spinning off
in all directions.
Foul ball! What else
could I call it?

The bat was real.

BLUES AT BREAKFAST
Adapted by John Hersey from his novel Blues

For many years I have been catching bluefish off the island where I live. These fish grow to be three feet long and to weigh as much as eighteen pounds, but most of the ones I catch weigh about five pounds. I have always wondered just what they looked like underwater when they were feeding. One day last winter in the Key West public library, I watched a film of some blues having their breakfast in a huge tank. The movie had been made by some scientists who were studying the habits of these wild and strong fish.

After all my years of fishing for blues and trying to see in my mind's eye what must have been happening under the surface—under the mirror of the sky—I was finally able, sitting there in a house of books, to feel as if I was going right into the sea with six blues, entering into their watery home and swimming with them.

At first we were in the dark of breaking dawn. The fish swam together in a school, paddling gently and coasting. They went their rounds. It grew lighter. The pace quickened. Then the blues began to hunt. The school broke; each was on its own. The great forked tails drove the fish faster and faster. You could see the huge engines of their body muscles working. The fish seemed to be made of flexible steel. The shading of their bodies made them look one solid submarine color not much different from that of the water—except for a bright spot, almost like a small round window lit from inside, at the forward base of the fin on each side, in back of the gills. Was this spot a way each fish could know other blues from a distance in the shadows of their world?

For a time the film went into slow motion. As each blue drifted past me, the angry eye on the near side swung like a loose button to focus on me, watching to see if I would attack it. Then, as the fish surprised and relieved me by calmly sailing along, the button swung farther forward. This was hunger time. I would not be good to eat, or even worth judging. One fish opened its mouth and moved its tongue, as if trying to test whether there were any signs of baitfish—or perhaps a bad taste of human beings around.

The film broke back to full speed, and the blues, on the alert, were whizzing past me like shooting stars in an August sky. Suddenly the smooth bright lid of our universe was broken in several places, as a handful of mummichogs were tossed into the tank from above and swam down from the surface. These were chubby four- and five-inch light-brown fish, with dark bars along their sides. They didn't get to swim far. The great bodies of the blues flashed up from below, like rockets, their powerful tails driving so hard they seemed to flutter. They were going so fast that they had to open their mouths two or three feet before they reached the bait—and how wide those saw-edged jaws stretched! Then the doom chop of razor teeth and a sudden sharp swerve to right or left, and a spurt down to be ready at once to kill again. More mummichogs. All around me there was a dreadful energy of powerful missiles, almost always shooting upward to keep the targets framed against the morning light. Sometimes the charging silver-gray parcels broke the shining surface overhead and then cut away downward, leaving a wobbling and bubbling ring of turmoil up there. Soon there began to be what looked like a snowfall of bits of bait, chopped away from what had been gulped, drifting toward the bottom. Other pieces, floating, speckled the surface.

It was all happening so fast—far faster than I can tell it to you—that it took me a while, with the help of some more slow motion, to notice two important things. One was that as the fish charged the bait, their eyes swung far forward. Even though the bright buttons were fastened to the sides of their heads, they appeared able to look straight ahead at the bait with both eyes. This meant that they could tell how far away they were from their food. So apparently sight—speed of eyes—was vital. Once, two blues saw the same mummichog at what seemed the same moment and rose in beautiful parallel leaps. But one's eyes must have been part of a second faster than the other's, and it got to the food first, breaking away to the right as the other, beaten, broke away just as fast to the left.

The other thing I saw was mysterious to me—and even scientists are baffled by it: As the fish fed, they kept flashing the two fins under their bodies at the forward end of their bellies. Most of the time, while swimming, they kept these two fins tucked up tight. But on the charge, while feeding, they kept dropping them all the way down, like fans opening. But very fast. The word for this had to be "flashing," because the transparent fins picked up the dawn light and shone like quick, bright signal flags.

Gradually, as the fish kept rising like fountain spray and as they began to feel full—which I thought would never happen—the upward surges went on but seemed to lose, bit by bit, their murderous urgency. The signals of the flags were less frantic. The huge propellers of the tails eased their drive. Not a single mummichog swam free of its fate; there always seemed to be room in some mouth for just one more. But the ceremony was working itself out.

Finally, the morning meal was over. The fish slowed their pace to normal cruising speed. Having competed with each other like athletes in the Olympics, to the limit of their strength, they now shaped up and went back to school. I must say, though, that at this point they looked more like teachers than pupils, with their rounded tummies and their calm air as if they were walking around with other teachers after school, and their look of having known all along that things would be this way.

A PACKAGE OF FISH

◆§ David Ignatow

We had bought the car for twenty-five bucks to give ourselves a joyride out of the steaming city to exotic places. Never before had we visited Sheepshead Bay.

I remember the bay and the fish smell, the wharves and the small wooden houseboats that sold fresh-caught fish; and the people in jeans and sun hats, hands callused from oars and fishing nets, faces tanned and toughened from the sun and spray and work, leaning against the rails of the houseboats, waiting for customers.

We were a carload of boys on a ride to see the waterfront of Brooklyn, where the bay leads out into the ocean. The people living there looked ready for any season, cold or hot, wet or dry, dull or busy. We looked and wondered why they would want to live in unclean-looking boats and fishy-smelling clothes.

Nearby were broken old hulks and cars abandoned on the pebbly sand, along with broken bottles and crumpled paper bags. We passed a stretch of flat gray stagnant water, the inlet of the bay. We wondered about it, as we thought how beautiful it was, with the sky free of buildings and the air strong and fresh.

We stopped at a boat to buy some fish—at least that

was our excuse. We wanted to look and talk and savor all this strange way of living. A smell of frying fish coming from the cabin hung around us. A man with a narrow face and a long bony nose, with hard thin lips and bright blue eyes stood at the rail of the boat. He asked if we'd come to buy.

We boys looked at one another, not wanting to finish the sale so quickly, wanting a chance to talk. One of us spoke up. "What kind do you have to sell?"

The water below stank like rotting cabbage leaves, motor oil, and stale fish, but we loved it. The houseboat was dirtier and older than it had appeared from a distance. The deck looked slippery and black from fish grease. The wooden slats of the cabin were splintered by rot from sea weather, but we were more impressed because of it, feeling more full of wonder than before that a man and his crew would want to live in such a place.

"We have bass, just caught this mornin', and some mackerel. Which do you want?"

The man was studying us for the answer. But we still had not found out all we wanted to know about this kind of living. It seemed both beautiful and ugly, and so we stalled by asking his advice.

"Mackerel are for frying, and bass make good soup, boys. Now which do you want?"

"We'll take both!" we said, almost with one voice. He smiled at our reply, and disappeared into the cabin.

"Can we come aboard and look around?"

"Come right up," he answered from inside. We

rushed up the shaky wooden steps that led to the deck. The sky was solid blue, and the air seemed more salty than before.

In the cabin stood racks of fishing poles, lined up in order according to size. Three cots with mussed-up sheets and blankets stood against the walls. There was a small radio, and a table with apple peelings on it, and plates with the remains of food, now covered with feasting flies. The walls were unpainted. A bare electric bulb hung on a cord from the ceiling.

The man had lifted a hatch in the floor and gone down a flight of stairs. We called below to ask if we could follow. The answer was yes, muffled by the walls and the distance. From below came the strong smell of live fish. One by one we went down the slippery steep stairs, carefully, into the cool shadows. Another bulb lit up the darkness somewhat by a hazy glow. In a dim corner, the man bent over a pile of fish.

"Is it a big one you want?" he asked, pulling one out of the heap by the tail.

"Sure," we answered together.

"This is like a fish store on the ocean!"

"Yeah?" said the man, slinging two fish onto a bench, where a knife and old fish scales lay.

"Do you live here too?" we asked.

"Uh-huh," he answered. "Want it gutted?"

"Sure!" we answered quickly, wondering what we were going to do with the fish and how much it would cost us. "You live here all the time?" we went on.

"All the time?" the man asked, puzzled.

"In the winter?" we added. "When it's cold?"

"Yeah," was the answer.

"You sell fish in the winter?"

"In the winter? Sure; all the time," he replied. He had scraped the fish and was wrapping it in old newspapers.

"But it must be cold here in the winter," one of us said.

"Sure, and I got a stove in the winter," he replied. "What's the matter? You boys looking to be fishermen?" he asked with a grin. "You won't like it. You have to live with lots of muck and slime. Do you want that?"

"Sure, why not?"

"Okay, then get to work," he said. "Clean some fish for me to fry so I can sell. Take 'em in your hands, and bring them upstairs like that!"

"Oh, no!" We laughed. No hard work for us! We were dressed up and out for fun. "Is that all you have for us to do?"

"That's all," he said. "One dollar and fifty cents for the fish," he added in a dry voice, holding the package of fish out to us.

We searched our pockets for the money, each trying to give no more than his exact share, knowing that now we had fish none of us knew what to do with. Finally, the money was fairly collected, and we presented it to the fisherman as a handful of coins. He took it and dropped it down into his side pocket.

He was getting ready to go up on deck again. We didn't want to lose him that fast. Maybe fishing was the thing we would enjoy out of all this.

"We could help you fish," one of us suggested.

"Okay, get up at four in the morning in the dark and put on your clothes and come along."

"Oh, no!" we cried in horror at the idea of breaking sleep in pitch dark. It might be bitter cold, and we would be leaving a warm bed, perhaps to meet the danger of the sea in the dark, while we were still sleepy. Not for us. Far from it.

The fisherman laughed, and passed us on his way to the ladder to the deck above. We followed close behind him, unwilling to be left in the shadowy, smelly gloom with fish scales, knives, and a blood-covered bench.

We entered the cabin, disheartened at the outcome of our adventure. "Then what is the fun in working here," we complained, gathering around him again as he stood by the stove and fried fish, "if it's so hard?"

"It's work, that's all."

"But what's the good of it!"

"That's what I say, kids, what's the good? It's just for the money."

"Just for the money?" we repeated unhappily.

"That's right, just for the money.

We scratched our heads in puzzlement and filed out of the cabin, the package of fish now one of us. "Goodbye," we called back.

"Goodbye," came the answer, flat and no longer interested.

Another car was pulling up to the water's edge, filled with new customers. We got into our car and started off. The breeze made by the speed was cooling in the hot sun, and it was pleasant. We were glad to be where we were, instead of in the cabin, or in a ship's gloomy bottom with a heap of live fish. We were glad not to be the man and have to do all that work on a filthy boat.

We were passing houseboats advertising fried oysters, lobsters, clams, and deep sea bass. Abandoned boat wrecks, tilted on their sides, and wrecked cars lined the beach. The blue sky still was clear of buildings, and the air had a strong smell of fish and salt that picked up our spirits.

We had to swear among ourselves that we could not understand. Somehow as we were riding, just as in the beginning, the scene was beautiful again, and we were wondering what the secret of it could be. We were still longing to know.

We got to the city, with its hotbox rooms piled on top of each other like so many packing crates, and we inserted ourselves, each into his own crate, to sweat out the night. Home again.

CLEANING A BASS

Ted Kooser

She put it on the chopping block
and it flopped a little, the red rick-rack
of its sharp gills sawing the evening air
into lengths, its yellow eyes like glass,
like the eyes of a long-forgotten doll
in the light of an attic. "They feel no pain,"
she told me, setting the fish upright,
and with a chunk of stovewood
she drove an ice pick through its skull
and into the block. The big fish curled
on its pin like a silver pennant
and then relaxed, but I could see life
in those eyes, which stared at the darkening
world of the air with terrible wonder.
"It's true," she said, looking over at me
through the gathering shadows, "they feel no
  pain,"
and she took her Swedish filleting knife
with its beautiful blade that leaped and flashed
like a fish itself, and with one stroke
laid the bass bare to its shivering spine.

MYRTLE

◄§ Ted Kooser

Wearing her yellow rubber slicker,
Myrtle, our *Journal* carrier,
has come early through rain and darkness
to bring us the news.
A woman of thirty or so,
with three small children at home,
she's told me she likes
a long walk by herself in the morning.
And with pride in her work,
she's wrapped the news neatly in plastic—
a bread bag, beaded with rain,
that reads WONDER.
From my doorway I watch her
flicker from porch to porch as she goes,
a yellow candle flame
no wind or weather dare extinguish.

ERIC'S LOVE

*⋙ Adapted by Lois Ruby from her story
"Something from the Dead Letter Office"*

Twelve-o-four Brookside didn't face the street but sat on the corner at an angle, like a girl at a dance hoping for a partner. Oh yes, the very house at 1204 Brookside, with its flowering trees and its dainty yellow trim, was sweetly feminine to Eric Melton Coburn.

Eric covered his route on foot and knew all the houses; he had been delivering mail to them almost half his life. He could spot mail-order packages in plain brown wrappers, traffic tickets, Social Security checks, sweepstakes entries, doctor bills. He knew when the babies came, and the divorces. And he knew just when Sam Barkett moved out of 1204. When Eric read Barkett's change-of-address cards, he printed the new California address in his own book. For three weeks after Sam had packed up and left, Eric noticed that his wife, Elizabeth, was still in her robe at eleven in the morning when she came to the door for her mail.

However, Mrs. Barkett wasn't his main interest at 1204. Terry was. When the Barketts first moved to Brookside, in Eric's tenth year on the route, Terry was only about thirteen—a slim, dark-eyed girl with long brown hair and a serious smile. She sent away for things like Christmas cards to sell, photos of movie stars, and, once, seeds of a plant that was supposed to grow without water or light. It was guaranteed on the outside of the package. Now Eric imagined a giant fern shading Terry's front bedroom upstairs.

Later, Terry wrote to pen pals all over the map: Sweden, Canada, Wyoming. What a stamp collection she must have! That summer there was more mail than he could fit into the box. So Eric would ring the bell and wait for Terry to tumble down the stairs.

"Oh, hi," she'd say, brushing her hair back over her ears.

He wished she would be more careful about opening the door to strangers.

"Nice day, Miss Barkett."

"Is it really? I haven't been out yet."

She was already fifteen. Barefoot and lean as an athlete in her blue jeans and a soft T-shirt, she would shade her eyes like an Indian scout and stick her big toe out onto the sunny porch, as if she were testing bathwater.

"Well, here's the mail," Eric would say, searching his mind for more important conversation.

"Is *all* that mail for me?" She pulled back her head and fluttered her brown eyes.

"I really couldn't tell you."

Would she play with him this way if she didn't like him? He handed her the mail, one piece at a time, watching her read the return addresses, then toss each letter carelessly onto the cluttered table in the hall. Why wasn't she tearing open the letter from the boy in Sweden? Eric would be willing to listen if she wanted to read parts of it to him. But no, she was gone in an instant, back to whatever it was that kept her inside all summer. Sometimes he would have to pull the front door shut himself.

Between that summer of pen pals and the fall of college catalogs, Eric admitted to himself that he was in love. He sized up his chances. He wasn't a bad-looking man. He, too, was lean and tall. His height was in his legs, strong and muscular from walking. In the summer he proudly wore the Bermuda shorts of his uniform. But no one ever remarked on what he wore. He was as unnoticeable in the neighborhood as a fire hydrant. It was his dull uniform, he told himself, not his face, which was boyish and blushed too easily. Also he knew he had special eyes, eyes that turned colors depending on how cloudy or clear the sky was, eyes that spoke for him when the words wouldn't come. No, he thought, it had to be the uniform. So he perked it up with holly sprigs in winter or a daisy in his buttonhole in summer. In the fall he tucked a rust-colored handkerchief in his breast pocket.

"What's that sticking out of your pocket?" Terry Barkett asked one day.

"Oh, this?" He blushed and stuffed the handkerchief down out of sight. She yanked it out of his pocket, and it floated off on the November wind. He did not chase after it.

"I'm just terrible," Terry said, holding back a laugh with her small fingers. "I'm really and truly sorry," she said, trying for all she was worth to *look* sorry.

That night at home, Eric relived the moment. She had reached out to him, had touched him, had taken something from him in a very personal way. And he had made her laugh. These were wonderful signs. Anything was possible now.

Eric had had very little experience with women. At an age when most men were teaching their sons to ride a bicycle, Eric hadn't even considered marriage. There was one woman at the postal station, but she was built like a wrestler and had a rough mouth on her. She was hardly a lady, Eric thought, compared to his Terry.

There had been no one before Terry, or since. She had been enough. It was enough to have watched her unfold from the girl collecting movie star photos to the young lady in jeans and bare feet, and finally into the woman who drove the white Volvo parked on Brookside.

Shortly after the Volvo appeared on Brookside, Eric noticed changes in the Barketts' mail. More letters were going to and coming from Sam Barkett in California. Travel folders from Jamaica and the Grand Canyon filled the mailbox. Letters arrived from the Hilton Hotel catering service and from the After Six Shop. Then one day about 150 large blue envelopes, neatly tied together, were hung on the hook of the box for him to mail. Eric set the bundle respectfully in his leather pouch and left in its place another copy of *Modern Bride*.

Terry was getting married.

After a week or so, small blue envelopes began trickling in. Eric checked the return addresses to see who had been invited to the wedding. Soon packages from fancy stores filled his mail pouch. Eric knew that Terry was home now on Saturdays, but he couldn't make himself ring the bell and hand her the gifts. He just opened the screen door and set them inside.

That winter was as cold and bleak as any Eric could remember. Harsh winds whipped his face as he shivered in his long, baggy uniform coat. After work it took half an hour in the shower for him to warm up. Later, wrapped in his thick, comfortable robe, Eric would tuck himself into bed and settle down with the newspaper. One evening there she was:

Teresa Barkett, daughter of Elizabeth Barkett of 1204 Brookside and Samuel Barkett of Los Angeles, California, to wed Dr. Michael Hoyt . . .

Eric's eyes misted, but he was able to finish:

. . . will be united in marriage on Saturday at Christ the King Lutheran Church.

So soon? She was barely twenty-one!

The reality of the situation struck him full force for

the first time. What had gone wrong? He thought their courtship was proceeding so well—before the blue envelopes had appeared. She had certainly smiled at him, and then there was the day she had taken his handkerchief. . . . He turned over and buried his face in the pillows.

The newspaper hadn't mentioned the time of the wedding, so by seven-thirty on Saturday morning Eric was dressed in his good suit and a navy-blue tie held at the third button by a pearl tie tack. He sat in his car in the parking lot across from Christ the King.

Four hours later, the white Volvo arrived. Sam Barkett, tanned and looking surprisingly young, Eric noted with a start, opened the car door for Terry as if she were a princess. Elizabeth Barkett had come round from the other side of the car to lift Terry's gown off the pebbles of the parking lot as her father guided her by the elbow into the church.

Guests began pulling into the lot. Eric joined the crowd crossing the street to the church. At the door, a smiling girl forced a pen into his hand and pointed to the guestbook. "Please," she said. He signed his name, *Eric Melton Coburn*, and took a seat on the bride's side of the church.

The familiar organ music began, and Terry swept up the aisle. Although she held her father's arm, it was clear that she was leading. Eric felt an urge to protest as Dr. Michael Hoyt bent to kiss the bride even before her father had given her away. The couple held hands all through the ceremony.

Afterwards, Eric stood in the receiving line. Just as Sam Barkett was ready to shake his hand, Terry glanced over at Eric and caught his eye. She stood on her tiptoes and whispered something to the groom, who gave Eric a searching look, then shrugged. Now Sam Barkett was patting Eric's back and passing him along to Elizabeth.

"Congratulations, Mrs. Barkett," Eric murmured, taking her hand in both of his. She smiled warmly, but her hand was freezing.

"Thank you, thank you," she said. "Sorry, I didn't quite catch your name?"

"Eric Melton Coburn."

"Ben, this is Eric Merton," she shouted, passing him on to the groom's parents.

"Martin!" Mr. Hoyt said, greeting him as if he were a member of the family. "Hannah," he said to his wife, "this is our Terry's Uncle Martin."

Then Eric was standing in front of Terry. His heart began to race as it had that day she pulled the handkerchief from his pocket.

"Hi," Terry said. "Glad you made it." She held out her hand. Her gold ring felt solid in his palm.

Did he dare do what all the others had done, men and women both? He leaned forward and brushed Terry's cheek with a kiss. Her cheek was as warm as his lips.

Terry turned her face toward her husband. "Mike,

this is— Oh, Aunt Mary!" The woman behind Eric had grabbed Terry and was spinning her around. Eric was left with Dr. Michael Hoyt.

"Good to see you," said the groom, taking Eric's hand in a firm grip. "I hope we'll be seeing a lot of you after we get settled in." He blinked sincerely for a moment, then dropped Eric's hand, to prepare a different smile for Aunt Mary.

Turned loose in the crowd of strangers, Eric wanted to leave at once while Terry's sweet smell was still on his coat. Near the main doors, he passed a large table stacked with gifts. Eric pulled an envelope from his pocket and quickly slid it between the cliffs of boxes. It would be scooped up with the rest of the presents and dumped in the trunk of someone's car to be delivered to their new address after their honeymoon. Eric's message read:

Someone loves you, Teresa Barkett Hoyt.

On the table next to the gifts was a bowl of pink candied almonds and a tiny Lucite box, the kind Eric's mother had on the kitchen table for Sweet'n Low. This one held a stack of printed cards. Eric slipped some almonds and a card into his pocket. He closed the front door of the church quietly, as if there were a child sleeping inside.

Several blocks from the church, Eric pulled over to the curb and reached for the card in his pocket. Popping two almonds in his mouth, he read:

After March 24
Dr. and Mrs. Michael Hoyt will be at home at
61200 Pebblespring Road
Woodridge

There was no state and no zip code. Eric could just imagine the mess in the post office if wedding gifts came addressed this way.

Eric eased the car back into drive and headed for home to enjoy what was left of his weekend. He'd fix himself a Denver omelet, watch a movie in bed, read the paper, maybe catch a baseball game on TV, turn in early. Then, on Monday, he would check with the supervisor to see who had the Pebblespring route. With his seniority and good record, he felt sure the postal department would honor his request for a change.

A VERY ANCIENT SONG
John Hollander

That man seems like some sort of god: he's lying
On the couch there next to you, as your earring
Trembles in the light of the fire dying,
      Seeing and hearing

What you are and what you say, and I'm shaking
Too, like someone who is freezing and burning
Both at once. Or someone whose vivid waking
      Dreams keep returning.

Looking at you, something—I feel—is flowing
From your eyes to mine, and however much you
Look away now, all I think of is going
      Over to touch you.

EROTIC POEM

◄§ *Peter Meinke*

I am too embarrassed
to write an erotic poem for you:
suppose my mother read it, or your mother?
What would they think
if I listed the various parts
of our anatomies
that work so well together?
What would they think
of this position or that place;
the look on your face just before,
the feeling I have just after?
I think I may have to wait
until our mothers are gone

and by then it may be too late.

In the meantime,
baby,
you turn me on.

I WONTA THANK YA

◦§ Tejumola F. Ologboni

God
you aint
made life no
easy thang
but I wonta
thank ya
for my
Black Woman

scoldin me
soothin me
soft voice
warm wind
huggin me
holdin me
my Queen
showin me
how to be the King
I used to
be

When I couldnt give her
nuthin
she returned a smile
when I done wrong
she forgave me more
than all your
pale angels
And when I couldnt
believe
in
you,
I could believe
in my
Black Woman

They put my
sweet sable woman
through
the hardness
of hell . . .
but to look
in her
soft
brown
eyes
aint nobody could tell

lovin me
movin me

evening star
ebony shadows
night bird
cricket song
soft grass
warm wind
dark
deep
skin
like the
summernight
sky

M
M
Mmm
good
woolly
hair
small warm
round breasts
inviting
thighs
and arms
flat smooth belly
like the grasslands
and the rhythm
of Africa in her fluid hips
full fine lips

like ripe purple plums
that grow only
at the
top
of the tree

oooweee!
my
Black Woman

even when she call me
baby
make me feel like a
Man
rubs my work-weary back
like no other woman can

God
you aint
made life no
easy thang,

but I wonta
thank ya
for
my
Black
Woman

QUEEN FOR A DAY

⋰ *Adapted by Russell Banks*
from his story "Queen for a Day"

Earl turns from the dimly lit worktable where he is writing. He waits a second, then says to his brother, "Hey, cut that out, will you! Get your feet off the walls."

"You can't tell me what to do," says the other boy. He is a dark-headed, moody ten-year-old, lying on his cot with his sneakers slapped up against the faded wallpaper. "You're not the boss of this family."

Earl stares at his brother. "We're supposed to be doing homework, you know. If she hears you tramping your filthy feet up the walls, she'll be in here screaming. So get your damned feet down. I'm not kidding."

"She can't hear me. Besides, you're not even doing homework. And *I'm* reading."

The older boy sucks his breath through his front teeth and glares. "Look, twerp, just get your goddamned feet down, will you? I can't concentrate, with you rubbing your feet all over the wallpaper." He turns back to his work. He is writing with a ballpoint pen on a sheet of lined notebook paper. Earl is a scrawny, muscular boy grown suddenly tall for his age, making him a head taller than George, taller even than their mother; tall enough to pat his sister's head, as if he were a full-grown adult.

Earl turned twelve eight months ago, in March, and in May their father left them. Their father is a union carpenter who worked on government projects all over the state and came home only on weekends. Then, every other weekend. Finally, he was gone for a month. When he came home that last time it was to say goodbye to Earl, George, and their sister, Louise.

And to their mother too, of course, though she had been saying for months now that she never wanted to see the man again anyhow, because he just caused trouble. He might as well stay away for good, she says. They can all get along better without him. Yes, that's true, Earl thought. But that was before the man had taken off and stopped sending them money. Now, six months later, Earl is no longer sure that they can get along better without their father than with him.

He left them on a Sunday morning. Their mother had called them from their rooms in a tight, angry voice. "Come out here! Your father has something important to say to you."

They gathered in a line before their father, who sat at the kitchen table, a pair of suitcases beside him, and in front of him a cup of coffee. His eyes were red and watery, the way they always were on Sunday mornings from his drinking the night before. On this Sunday morning it was a little worse than usual. His hands shook so that he could barely hold his cigarette. He kept busy stirring his coffee while he talked. He had trouble looking his children in the face.

"Your mother and me," he said in a strange, low voice, "we decided some things you children should know." He cleared his throat. "Your mother, she thinks you ought to hear it from me, though I don't know about that, since it isn't completely my idea alone." He studied his coffee cup for a few seconds.

"They should hear it from you because it's what you *want!*" their mother cried out. She stood by the sink wringing her hands, glaring at him. Her face was swollen and red from crying, which was not an unusual thing to see when their father was home.

"Adele, it's *not* what I want," he said. "It's what's got to be, that's all. Kids," he said, "I got to leave you for a while. And I won't be coming back, I guess." He grabbed his cigarette, inhaled the smoke fiercely, and went on as if he were talking to the table: "I don't want to do this, but I got to. It's hard to explain, although I think someday you'll all understand. I just . . . just got to live somewhere else now."

Louise, the six-year-old, was the only child who could speak. "Where are you going, Daddy?"

"Upstate," he said. "Back up to where I been all along. I got me an apartment up there, a small place."

"That's not all he's got up there!" their mother said.

"Adele, I can walk out of here right this second if you keep up with that kind of stuff."

Earl asked, "Will . . . will you come and see us? . . . Or can we come visit you, on weekends and like that?"

"Sure, son, you can visit me anytime you want. It'll take me a while to get the place set right, but soon as I get it all set up for kids, I'll call you and we'll work out some nice visits. I won't be coming here, though, you understand."

Earl shook his head up and down to show that he understood, and as if his only concern had now been put to rest.

George turned his back on his father and, taking tiny half steps across the kitchen linoleum, headed toward the door. Nobody tried to stop him, because he was doing what all of them wanted to do. They heard him running, almost falling down the two flights of stairs to the front door of the building. The door slammed and they knew he was gone, running between parked cars, down the alley, to a hiding place where he would stop, sit, and bawl. They knew it because they wanted to do it themselves, especially Earl, who was too old, too scared, and too confused to cry. Instead of running away, Earl said, "I hope everyone can be more happy now."

His father looked at him for the first time. "Hey, son"—he smiled—"you're the man of the house now. I know you can do it . . . and listen, I'm proud of you. Your mother, the kids . . . they're all going to need you a hell of a lot more than they have before. I'm counting on you." He stood up and rubbed out his cigarette. Then he reached past Earl to hug Louise. He lifted her off her feet and squeezed her tight. When he set her down, he wiped tears away from his eyes. "Tell Georgie . . . Well, maybe I'll see him downstairs or something. He's upset, I guess. . . ." He shook Earl's hand, gave him a quick hug, and let go. Grabbing up his suitcases without once looking over at his wife or back at his children, he left the apartment for good.

"And good riddance too," their mother said to anyone who would listen.

For a day or so, Louise said she missed her daddy. Then she seemed to forget the man who had worked away from home most of her life. George stayed mad, deep inside himself, and said nothing at all.

Earl did not know how he felt about their father's abandoning them; in some ways it was the best thing he could have done, and in other ways it was the worst. Earl started to speak of him as if he had died in an accident and had left their mother a widow, and his children half orphaned.

Earl began to concentrate on survival for them all, which he now understood to be his personal responsibility. His mother seemed hardly able to manage, and his brother and sister, of course, were still babies. Often, late at night, lying on his narrow cot, Earl would say to himself, "I'm the man of the house now." Somehow, just saying it, over and over like a prayer, made the terror less, and he could finally sink into sleep.

In their first six months alone, their mother is badly shaken and cannot find her balance. It is as if her husband were abandoning her over and over again: agreeing to send money, then sending nothing; promising to call and write letters, and then going silent on them; planning visits, but leaving them without even an address.

Earl feels more and more that it is up to him to hold things together. He lies on his cot thinking up schemes to replace their lost father. His best idea is to introduce his mother to his hockey coach, but he, surprisingly, turns out to have a wife and even a new baby. Then Earl invites the cigar-smoking deliveryman who drops off the newspapers he must deliver before school to come in for breakfast and to meet his mom. But the man tells Earl, "No thanks, kid. I'm sure your ma is a nice lady, but I got no use for any of 'em is why I'm single. Not because I ain't met the right one yet."

After a few more tries, Earl turns his thoughts to more dignified plans: sweepstake and lottery tickets, which he buys with his paper route money. He enters essay and jingle writing contests, even a spelling bee. A prize, any kind of award or notice from the world outside, Earl believes, will make their mother happy and set the course of their new life. Somehow it will separate them once and for all from their father, as if he had never existed.

"So what are you writing now?" George demands from his cot. He walks his feet up the wall as high as he can reach. "What is it, a *love* letter?" He goggles his eyes. "Let's see!" He stands and makes a grab for the paper.

"You little sonofabitch," Earl says, grabbing back, pulling George forward onto the floor, where they start swinging. In a minute, the door of their room is opened. "Get up, both of you," their mother screams. "I can't *stand* it when you fight, you know that. I can't *stand* it!"

Earl gets to his feet and says, "Sorry, Ma," and gently turns her around and steers her back to the living room, which is dark except for the light of the television. "We'll be out soon and watch with you," he says. He scoops up the mess of papers and pens they have dragged to the floor. "Here, nosy. Want to see what I was writing? Go ahead, look, I don't care."

"I don't care, either, unless it's a *love* letter."

Dear Jack Bailey,
I think my mother should be Queen for a Day because she has suffered a lot and has come out of it very cheerful and loving. The fact is, my father left her alone with us three children and has gone to live with some other woman. He has been gone more than six months

now. *The lawyer to get us support money says he will need $50, but we don't have that much.*

Also, my father left our car here because he took the pickup. But he still owed $450 on the car, so the bank took it back. Now our mom has to walk everywhere and carry things and that makes big blue veins in her legs that hurt. The rest of the time she is cheerful.

That is why I believe that this woman, my mother, should be Queen for a Day.

> *Sincerely,*
> *Earl Painter*

Earl knows it is not easy to become a contestant. First, your letter has to appeal to Jack Bailey. Then your mom has to be able to show her suffering over television in a dramatic way. Earl supposes that when he receives this letter, Jack Bailey will write, or maybe telephone, to invite him and his mother to come to New York City to tell her story in person. Then, when Jack Bailey chooses her and two other nominees, they will all come back, probably the next week, to tell their stories live on television. At night, in his dreams, Earl sees his mother smiling as she is crowned "Queen for a Day."

Several weeks slide by, and Earl does not receive the letter he expects. He thinks all the time about the *Queen for a Day* television show and the sad stories the contestants tell Jack Bailey about their illness, poverty, and plain bad luck. The studio audience is moved to tears. Then everyone cries again and claps when the winning victims are rewarded with refrigerators, living room suites, vacation trips, and, if they need it, twenty-four-hour nursing care. Earl feels these women's lives aren't much different from his own mother's. Probably his mother's life is worse.

When Earl gets home after hockey practice, he asks Louise and George if there is any mail for him, any letter. "You're sure? Nothing? No phone calls, either?" Earl heads for the bedroom and flops onto his bed, face first. He wishes he could keep falling, like down a bottomless mine shaft, into darkness, to be lost and, finally, blameless. Gone, gone.

Soon he is asleep.

Later, while George, Louise, and their mom watch television in the living room, Earl sits at his worktable and writes:

Dear Jack Bailey,

Maybe my first letter about why my mother should be Queen for a Day did not reach you. But I thought I should write again anyway to mention a few new developments. My mother got fired from her job on account of having nervous spells a lot these days because of my father and us kids and all.

I know that lots of people are poor as us, and many of them are crippled from polio or are blind, but I still think my mother should be Queen for a Day because of

other things. Even though she got fired and has dizzy
spells, and my father left, she stays here and takes care
of us children.

Thank you very much for considering Adele
Painter, my mother, to be Queen for a Day on television.
                                        Sincerely,
                                        Earl Painter.

It is dark now. The little kids have gone out to
the Christmas pageant at St. Joseph's. Earl is checking
the icebox for milk, when his mother comes in and
sits at the kitchen table. They are silent for a minute,
then she says, "I been talking to Father LaCoy, Earl.
You know, about . . . problems. I been asking his advice, and he says that your father and me, we should
try to get together."

"And you think he's right?"

"Well, not exactly. But he told me it's wrong for us
to go on like this, without a father and all. He told me
he'd like to set up a meeting between us so we could
maybe talk some of our problems out,"

"Yeah, but how come Father LaCoy thinks . . . How
can he even find . . . Listen, Ma, Daddy doesn't *want* us!"

"I know, I know," his mother murmurs. "But what
can I do? What else can I do?" She looks up at her son.
There is a new hardness in her face. She tells him, "You
don't understand. You must try to understand how it's
been for me too. I . . . can't go on like this."

Earl is nearly a full head taller than his mother, but

now, for the first time since his father left, he feels small again, like a child, helpless, pulled this way and that by the mysterious needs and desires of adults.

"Do you love Daddy?" he demands. *"Do* you, Ma? Ma, he *left* us!"

Earl is weeping now, his skinny arms wrapped around his own chest, tears streaming over his cheeks. "I *hate* him! I *hate* him, and I *never* want him to come back. If you let him come, I swear it, I'm gonna run away!"

"Oh no, Earl, you don't mean that. You don't hate your father"

"Yes, Ma, I do. And you should hate him, too, after all he did."

They are silent for a moment, facing each other, looking into each other's pale-blue eyes. He and his mother have the same sad down-turning eyes, the same full red mouth, and now, at this moment, the same agony. "All right," she says at last. "I'll tell Father LaCoy I don't want to talk to your father. I'll say that it's all gone too far." She opens her arms and her son steps into them. Above her head, his eyes jammed shut, he holds his tiny mother and sobs, as if he has just learned that his father has died.

The Friday before Christmas, they are all sitting in the living room watching *The Jackie Gleason Show,* when the phone rings.

"You get it, George," Earl says.

"Get it yourself. I always get it, and it's never for me."

"Answer the phone, Louise," their mother says. Louise picks up the phone. Her face suddenly goes dark, then brightens, wide-eyed. Earl watches her, and he knows who she is talking to. She nods, as though the person at the other end can see her. After a moment, the child puts the receiver down gently. "It's Daddy," she tells them. "He says he wants to talk to the boys."

"I'm not going to talk to him," George says, and stares into the television.

Their mother opens and closes her mouth, looks from George to Louise, to Earl, then back to Louise again. "It's Daddy?" she says. "On the telephone?"

"Un-huh. He says he wants to talk to the boys."

"Earl?" his mother asks, eyebrows raised.

"Nope."

His mother walks slowly to the phone. "Nelson?" she says. She nods, listening, now and then opening her mouth to say something, but closing it as she is interrupted. "Yes," she says, "they're here." She listens again. "Yes, I know, but I should tell you, Nelson, the boys don't want . . . It's hard for them with the holidays and all. We're upset too, with me losing my job and . . ." She listens again, longer this time. "Well, wait a minute, I'll ask again." She puts her hand over the receiver and holds it out to Earl and meets his eyes. Silently the boy gets up and crosses the room to the phone.

"H'lo," he says.

"H'lo, son. How're ya doin', boy? Been a while, eh?"

"Yeah. Quite a while."

"Well, I sure am sorry for that, you know, but I been going through some hard times myself. Didn't work most of the summer because of the strike. Son, look, it's been tough all around, so I know what you been through. I want to make it up to you guys a little, you and George and Louise, if you'll let me. What do ya say?"

"Sure. Why not? Go ahead and try."

"Hey, listen, Earl, what's that attitude you got there? We've got to do something about that. I guess some things have changed around there since the old man left, eh? Eh?"

"Sure they have. What did you expect? Everything would stay the same?" Earl hears his voice breaking. His eyes fill with tears.

"No, of course not. I understand, son. We've all made mistakes this year. It's hard, Earl, to do things like that right. But hey, listen, everybody deserves a second chance, right? Even your old man?" He's turned over a new leaf, he says. The past is past. He wants to come over tomorow with a Christmas tree and some presents, just like in the old days. "Would you go for that, son?"

"Daddy?"

"Yeah, sure, son. What?"

"Daddy, are you going to try to get back together with Mom?"

"Well . . . that's a hard one, boy. You asked me a hard one." Earl can hear him sipping from a glass. He can hear the ice. "I'll tell you the truth, boy. The truth is she don't want me. I left because *she* wanted me to leave, son. Right from the beginning, this thing's been your mom's show, not mine."

"Daddy, that's a lie."

His father is silent for a minute. Then he says, "You sure have got yourself an attitude since I been gone. Listen, kid, there's lots you don't know anything about. You're a long way from being a man, Earl, so don't go butting in where you're not wanted between your mom and me that you can't understand. Just butt out. You hear me?"

"Yeah, I hear you."

"Let me speak to your brother."

"He doesn't want to talk to you," Earl says. He turns his back to the room.

"Put your mother on, Earl."

"None of us wants to talk to you."

"Earl!" his mother cries. "Let me have that phone!" She rises from the couch and reaches out.

Earl places the receiver in its cradle. Then he stands there looking into his mother's blue eyes, and she looks into his.

She says, "He won't call back."

Earl says, "I know."

THE WORDS ON THE PAGE,
THE WORLDS IN YOUR HANDS

◄§ Thomas M. Disch

I am a writer. I write novels for a living, and I also review them for newspapers and magazines. And sometimes I teach other people to write fiction. So you'd think I'd know all about *why* people love to read, and about what's happening in their heads when they read a story. But I don't even have a very clear idea what's going on in *my* head when I'm reading a novel. It's a bit like seeing a movie, but the picture isn't always very sharp. Sometimes reading a book can be like talking to a friend, or listening in on other people's conversations. But I think the closest thing to reading fiction is dreaming.

When you dream, you can see things you've never seen in real life. For instance, you can fly, in dreams, better than Superman. In dreams you can talk with your parents, who may have died or may be far away. You can sing, in dreams, like the best opera singer in the world, like Pavarotti, though in real life you may not be able to sing much better than you can fly.

In a nutshell, in dreams you can do anything you're able to imagine, and the same is true of reading novels. Take the first book I can remember reading, *The Call of the Wild,* by Jack London. Buck, the hero of that book, is a dog who is also half wolf—or a wolf who is half dog. Deciding which of those is the real truth for Buck is what the book is all about. Is he a wild beast, or is he tame? Man's best friend, or a deadly enemy? Buck grows up wild in the Yukon, the wildest, farthest-north part of Canada. He hunts and is hunted, until he gets caught by a trapper and is tamed and learns to pull a dog sled. As I turned the pages of the book, I felt Buck's blood in my veins. I felt his hunger, his need to hunt, his terror when he was hunted, and his panic when he was trapped. I was with Buck every step of the way.

No movie or TV show could ever have got me inside that wolf-dog's skin the way Jack London did. For one thing, they don't have the time. A movie is over in an hour or two. A good book is with you for days, even weeks, and it lives in your mind long after you've read the last page. That's because a book's story comes at you from deep inside the part of your mind where dreams come from. I *became* Buck when I read the book, just as easily as I can become, in my dreams, a mountain climber or a millionaire.

The Call of the Wild was just one book, just a single dream. Since then I have lived, as a reader of novels, a thousand other lives no less strange, no less real, no less wonderful and/or terrifying. And that is another way novels are like dreams: some of the best of them can be very upsetting. But somehow it's an upsetment you need.

As a novel-reader I've lived in Paris, in Mexican

jungles, and on most of the planets of this solar system and a few hundred others besides. (As you can tell, I've read a lot of science fiction.) I've fought in every war from the Revolutionary War to Vietnam. I've made love to some of the world's most beautiful women and have been driven mad by others. I've committed terrible murders (though I usually get caught), and from time to time I've even been a saint. I've died a thousand deaths, and I'm still alive to tell the tale.

I've also laughed my head off with Charles Dickens, one of the funniest English writers who ever lived. Dickens wrote books about life in London over a hundred years ago, though you'd think he had written them yesterday. The jokes are still that fresh. I've also cried a few buckets of tears with Charles Dickens. When you really get to know writers like Dickens, reading one of their books is like visiting a favorite aunt or uncle in another country.

Novels are not the most important thing in the world. They won't make a thin soup any thicker or fix a flat tire. They don't put money in your pocket. But I know that my own life would have been several sizes smaller without my imaginary visits to Jack London's Yukon and Charles Dickens's London.

I realize that I still haven't explained exactly how it works, how a string of words on a page can turn into a dream in your head that is as real as your own life. I can only tell you it is so, that it happens all the time. Just look around, and you'll see them all out there, in the supermarkets and bookstores and libraries, shelf after shelf of books, rack after rack of bright new novels. And each one is calling out: Read me. Dream me. Enter my world. Fly away.

COPYRIGHT ACKNOWLEDGMENTS